SCHOOL BUDGETING
for Hard Times

Confronting

Cutbacks

and

Critics

William K. Poston, Jr.

Foreword by Fenwick W. English

CORWIN
A SAGE Company

For information:

Corwin
A SAGE Company
2455 Teller Road
Thousand Oaks, California 91320
(800) 233-9936
Fax: (800) 417-2466
www.corwin.com

SAGE India Pvt. Ltd.
B 1/I 1 Mohan Cooperative
  Industrial Area
Mathura Road, New Delhi 110 044
India

SAGE Ltd.
1 Oliver's Yard
55 City Road
London EC1Y 1SP
United Kingdom

SAGE Asia-Pacific Pte. Ltd.
33 Pekin Street #02-01
Far East Square
Singapore 048763

Printed in the United States of America

Library of Congress Cataloging-in-Publication Data

Poston, William K.
School budgeting for hard times: confronting cutbacks and critics / William K. Poston, Jr.; foreword by Fenwick W. English.
  p. cm.
Includes bibliographical references and index.
ISBN 978-1-4129-9090-5 (pbk.)

  1. School budgets—United States. 2. Education—United States—Finance. I. Title.

LB2830.2.P67 2011
371.2′06—dc22   2010038703

This book is printed on acid-free paper.

10   11   12   13   14   10 9 8 7 6 5 4 3 2 1

Acquisitions Editor:	Hudson Perigo
Associate Editor:	Allison Scott
Editorial Assistant:	Lisa Whitney
Production Editor:	Amy Schroller
Copy Editor:	Ellen Howard
Typesetter:	C&M Digitals (P) Ltd.
Proofreader:	Gretchen Treadwell
Indexer:	Molly Hall
Cover Designer:	Michael DuBowe
Permissions Editor:	Adele Hutchinson

Contents

Foreword

Budget figures reveal far more about proposed policy than speeches.

U.S. President Harry S. Truman

I t would be hard to imagine a more timely book to confront the overwhelming gloom and doom atmosphere in which American education is currently shrouded than this one. The deep recession in the nation's financial heartland on Wall Street has prompted a search for funds to keep school systems afloat and avoid debilitating layoffs and reductions in basic educational programs. Today, school system administrators are considering such dire antidotes to fiscal exigencies as moving to a four-day work week, closing dozens of schools, furloughing or cutting back on teachers, and other drastic remedies once thought ill-advised in order to reduce costs to match shrinking revenues.

The lack of progress in advancing student achievement in the nation's inner city schools such as Kansas City and Detroit is resulting in greater pushes for privatization, and more critics saying that U.S. public education hasn't got any better despite billions of dollars spent to improve it. Such criticism ignores the fact that there is no national system of education in the United States, but rather fifty different systems of education and many subunits, called school districts, within each of those. It is here that we can locate the basic responsibilities for educating our children.

So readers should know that Bill Poston is an educator first and an educational financial analyst second. He is a former math and physics teacher, middle school principal, and superintendent of schools in Arizona and Montana. He has fought the budget wars and won most of them in his career. In the process, he conducted workshops and staff development sessions on performance-based budgeting all over the country. He was the executive director of the Iowa School Business Management Academy for over 15 years and a professor of educational administration for 15 years at Iowa State University in Ames, Iowa.

What makes Bill Poston different from other writers about school budgeting is that he has never "confused things of logic for the logic of things" (Bourdieu, 1998,

p. 101), meaning he understands that budgets are the means to educational ends and are not ends themselves. He also understands that budget priorities reflect the unique values held dear by Americans and are highly localized wherever Americans may live and work. So this book about performance-based budgeting is the means for locally elected or appointed boards of education and their superintendents to use the always scarce resources from taxes to attain more of their valued ends than before and avoid the dire cutbacks which threaten the viability and vibrancy of our local educational systems during these hard times.

The advice in this book is hard-earned wisdom—it's from an educator who has walked the walk. Bill Poston is not an armchair theorist or policy wonk writing in a think tank cubicle whose only connections to the real world are blogs, web pages and thin-aired theoretical arguments of esoteric quantitative mole hills. He's a former U.S. marine who is the youngest elected international president of Phi Delta Kappa in its history, and an administrator who has "been there." I've always admired how Bill keeps his feet on the ground and finds a way to teach through his wonderful stories he has collected over a long and distinguished career, and how he brings his experience home to make a difference for thousands of children, in classrooms all over America, who may never know his name, but who have benefited from his advice, caring, and hard-nosed compassion.

—Fenwick W. English

R. Wendell Eaves Senior Distinguished
Professor of Educational Leadership

School of Education, University of North
Carolina at Chapel Hill

Preface

BUDGETING: BALANCING COST EFFICIENCY AND EDUCATIONAL EFFECTIVENESS

A plethora of fiscal crises is clearly negatively impacting schools across the nation. Economic stress has proliferated globally in recent months, with financial reductions trickling down to cause stress and strain in individual school system budgets. Moreover, with political efforts to reduce the scope of government, including school systems, commentators and critics of public schools continue unabated in their assaults on tax revenues. Shortfalls, cutbacks, and retrenchment have emerged of late to threaten not only education itself but also the essential quality of schooling and human development for youth. The end does not appear to be in sight at the time of this writing. Coping with financial rollbacks and justifying educational programs and services in times of financial recession is no easy task. Although the work is challenging and time is fleeting, education can demonstrate quality to skeptics, exhibit fiscal prudence to taxpayers, and enhance productivity given suitable tools, processes, and confidence in the mutually beneficial relationship between schools and society.

This book seeks to provide the tools, procedures, and some insights into how productivity is enhanced within the prevailing context of limited resources and problematical decision making in resource allocations. Budgeting is the result of a number of actions taken in school systems, including the following:

- The determination of the resources the system may need and where it might use them
- The identification of where and how the system may derive revenues and funding
- The choices the system may make for using those revenues on programs, services, or matériel (i.e. equipment, apparatus, and supplies of an organization)
- The selection and execution of a decision-making process for allocating resources
- The demonstration of quality within the educational institutions despite limited resources and public gloom common in hard economic times

However, the challenge of budgeting doesn't end there. School leaders need to choose from several types of budgeting processes, to follow principles of quality enhancement with cost-benefit analysis, and to capitalize on the benefits of performance-based budgeting processes to get optimal productivity or "bang for the buck" and to assure their constituencies that confidence in the school system is not misplaced.

It is time for a change in school budgeting practices for a number of reasons. Most school administrators are aware of contemporary pressures caused by social-political forces that want schools to get better at what they do while at the same time expecting those improved results with the same or even less financial support. This anomaly persistently challenges educational leaders to meet often conflicting expectations.

Of course, school transformation and improvement activities have significant budget and management implications. In improving the effectiveness and quality of instruction, it is often necessary to make changes in operations without any corresponding increase in resources. The challenge is to improve the productivity of schools within existing, or even diminishing, resources. As one discerning teacher once said, "We need to do more with less." Educators have had to make do with little in the way of resources for generations, and have done remarkably well under the circumstances.

Moreover, budgeting for both quality and economy is not quite that simple, and school improvement calls for careful planning, particularly in the use of scarce resources. As educators work to budget financial, human, and technical resources for school quality enhancement, the focus of activity must be on *what needs to be achieved*, not what the organization plans to buy.

Performance-based budgeting is remarkably straightforward, but it is not commonly found in public schools across the country. It is a different paradigm, but it provides school systems with improved understandings of system needs, program and service initiatives, and ways and means of evaluating for system advancement in their core mission—teaching and learning. Performance-based budgeting is based upon some clear-cut—some might say common sense—principles, including the following:

- Budget making is not a plan—it is a financial mechanism to carry out an organizational plan.
- Closely held budget processes and closed governance are potentially corruptible. Transparency in budgeting is necessary for credibility and productivity.
- Participatory decision making is not the same as shared decision making, where decisions are "made and shared." It is decision making where participants are equals in formulating determinations.
- Participatory decision making leads to better information, decisions, understanding, and support.
- Tangible connections between costs and objectives are essential—what is gained or lost needs to be clearly evident with or without funding.

- Budget decision accountability demands evidence of results and performance, lucid validity of assertions and intentions, and demonstrated improvement in organizational outputs per unit of input.

The recent proliferation of fiscal crises is clearly negatively impacting schools across North America. This book offers practical strategies to overcome obstacles and constraints. It's a guide to doing more with less. It hopefully provides tools for school system leaders in confronting financial constraints, in surmounting organizational limitations, and in improving the quality of the educational enterprise.

On a final note, no book of any type is the exclusive product of one individual, and this book is no exception. First and foremost, I am eternally grateful for the blessings and encouragement I have received from my wife of nearly five decades, Marcia, and my supportive family—especially my daughters, Heather Boeschen and Holly Kaptain, who unselfishly contributed to the quality of this book.

It is important to note my gratitude for Sam Bliss, professor at Northern Arizona University, who piqued my curiosity in his book on zero-based budgeting—which is referred to in this book as incremental budgeting—and also appreciation for Gary Knox, my colleague in Billings, Montana, for three years, for sharing with me the concepts of zero-based budgeting he had used in Salem, Oregon, over 25 years ago. Most importantly, I am deeply grateful to Dr. Fenwick English, Distinguished Professor of Educational Leadership at the University of North Carolina, who spurred me to action in making sure the needs of curriculum and learning would drive the budgeting process, not the other way around.

Of course, I would be remiss not to express gratitude to many colleagues who steadfastly implemented the budgeting approach and provided constructive feedback, including David Shapley (Hopkins, Minnesota), Randy Stortz (Bay Village, Ohio), Milt Pippinger (Garden City, Kansas), Dave Suman (Osseo, Minnesota), Galen Howsare (West Des Moines, Iowa), Roger Anton (Salinas, California), Cole Pugh (Eagle Mountain-Saginaw, Texas), and Ben Picard (Sunnyvale, California).

Gratitude is also due to many, many others, too numerous to list here. And that sentiment underscores one of the philosophical underpinnings of the precept that "all of us are smarter than any of us." To my many friends and colleagues who have shared in and contributed to my professional growth and knowledge, I humbly offer my sincere thanks.

Acknowledgments

Corwin gratefully acknowledges the contributions of the following reviewers:

Randel Beaver
Superintendent
Archer City Independent School District
Archer City, Texas

David L. Flynn
Director of Commission on Public Elementary and Middle Schools
New England Association of Schools and Colleges
Bedford, MA

David Freitas
Professor
Indiana University, South Bend
Granger, Indiana

Gary Lee Frye
Director of Developments and Grants
Lubbock-Cooper Independent School District
Lubbock, Texas

R. Kieth Williams
Retired Public School Superintendent
Professor, Director of Educational Leadership
Harding University
Searcy, Arkansas

About the Author

William K. Poston, Jr., EdD is an Emeritus Professor of Educational Leadership and Policy Studies at Iowa State University in Ames, Iowa, where he served for 17 years. He began his educational career as a math and physics teacher, and he accumulated 25 years of experience in educational administration including 15 years as a superintendent in Tucson and Phoenix, Arizona, and in Billings, Montana.

Dr. Poston earned his BA degree at the University of Northern Iowa, and his EdS and EdD degrees at Arizona State University. He served in the United States Marine Corps from 1958 to 1961. He has many distinctive professional achievements, including service as the youngest-elected *international* president of Phi Delta Kappa, and selection as an Outstanding Young Leader in American Education in 1980.

Dr. Poston was the executive director of the Iowa School Business Management Academy—the licensure program for school business managers in Iowa—for 15 years. He is the originator of curriculum-driven budgeting, and he has led over 75 curriculum audits in the United States and other countries. He has written 13 books and over 40 journal articles and continues to provide extensive service to schools in the areas of evaluation, curriculum management auditing, performance-based budgeting, and organizational quality improvement.

Performance-Based Budgeting

Beginning the Journey

Connecting financial support for public schools with performance is nothing new. Over fifteen years ago, the National Institute on Educational Governance, Finance, Policymaking, and Management identified this issue as one of the key questions facing public education. The Institute raised the question, "How can school finance systems be linked to performance?" (Schwartz, 1997). Both policy makers and education leaders wanted sound information to help them budget for results and to judge program quality and expenditure cost-effectiveness. The need continues to this day.

INTRODUCTION

Most people, especially teachers, have learned to cope with occasions in their lives when funds available were not sufficient to provide all the things they needed in their work. Wants were clearly subordinate to needs, and teachers learned how to do without something until it became necessary and affordable. Somehow the choice was made with discriminating judgment, and at minimum, there was usually some rational decision-making process.

This hasn't always been the case with school systems. The process of budgeting often has trumped the rational needs of the instructional process by limiting expenses without regard to a sense of priorities in terms of the system's mission. An arbitrarily determined budget has constrained many education systems. Schools have often been given an amount of funding, and instructed to carry out the work of the system in delivery of learning.

This is not unlike a tailor or seamstress who has selected a pattern for a garment which requires a certain amount of fabric but the amount of fabric available is less than needed. If the seamstress chooses to go ahead and make the garment anyway, the result is likely a missing part of the garment, perhaps rendering it useless. So it is with schools—sometimes teachers and administrators are expected to cut the pattern to fit the cloth. The educational program is cut or shaped to fit within a budget, and frequently, quality suffers and some important things are left out.

For example, some school districts engage in long-range planning in order to identify emerging needs and to prepare for meeting them. Then another, often clandestine or closely held, planning (budgeting) process develops a different plan, which ignores the needs by fragmenting programs and services with "line-item" or cost accounting–based funding. Often, the budget plan trumps the needs-based organizational plan for financial reasons. It is virtually impossible for a school system to improve its quality and effectiveness over time given these circumstances.

A productive school system is one that gets better over time, independent of changes in the level of resources available to it. In other words, even if the school were declining in enrollment and financial support, it should be possible to improve performance given certain actions by the system. The trick is to use the tools at the disposal of the system to improve the effectiveness and quality of the school organization's operations and to improve the efficiency of its processes at the same time.

The Less Is More Conundrum

How can one make a school more educationally effective and at the same time more cost-efficient? It sounds like the impossible dream—getting better and doing more but doing it with less. In effect, it would be an exercise in improving productivity. There is a way to do that, which at first blush may appear counterintuitive.

Primarily, achieving greater productivity involves research-based systems characterized by accumulation of hard data, extrapolation of findings, and implementation of action accordingly. As a school organization plans, organizes, implements, and evaluates its activities, it can only get better if it makes adjustments or modifications in its activities as a result of feedback on its performance. If feedback is spotty, flawed, or ignored, productivity is jeopardized. If feedback is comprehensive, thorough, valid, and used in decision making, productivity is enhanced.

If a school organization establishes a solid tie-in between what it does and how well it does it, and then uses that link to shape what it does next, the organization normally will improve in performance. In addition, it should improve in its use of resources, reduce wasteful activity, terminate ineffective programs, and generally get better at what it does over time (Deming, 1986). It simply may end up doing less, but gaining greater effectiveness and improved results.

A Model for Productivity

One way to look at the development of productivity is by illustrating its components in graphic form, as shown in the following exhibit. In this illustration, a linear relationship among needs, mission, goals, objectives, methods, matériel, activities, and feedback is shown.

Steps to productivity in organizations include these nine components, in varying degree, and progression through specific procedures like these improves productivity. The key to success in improvement usually involves consideration of the steps.

Productivity Model

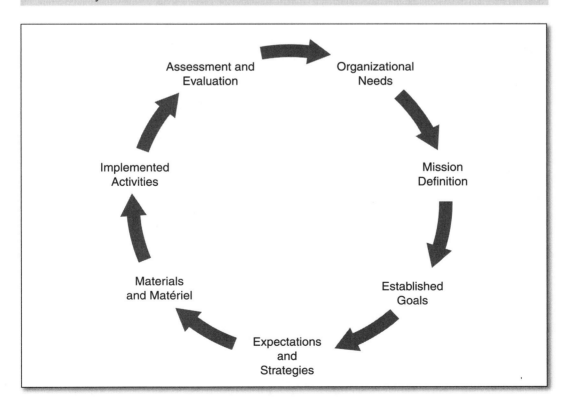

STEPS IN A TYPICAL LINEAR PROGRAM QUALITY CYCLE TO IMPROVE PRODUCTIVITY

1. Determine organizational needs, using appropriate needs assessment techniques.

2. Define the organizational mission or the overall results that are desirable or expected.

3. Establish organizational goals for the next three to five years.

4. Delineate organizational expectations and program objectives.

5. Identify and select from alternative methods and strategies that might be employed, including staffing.

6. Develop or select appropriate materials, equipment, or other matériel necessary to do the job.

7. Implement planned activities in accordance with organizational decisions to this point.

8. Assess or measure results and performance, and apply evaluative judgment.

9. Use feedback in determining organizational needs and cycle through the process again.

Cautions and Considerations

Some cautions should be noted here. This program quality cycle is considerably boiled down in complexity and scope. For more comprehensive direction in planning and decision making, consult more complete and useful information found in the References and the Additional Suggested Reading at the end of the References.

Some conditions for use of this simple decision-making cycle for productivity should also be noted. There are certain administrative precepts that need to be followed. For example, collaboration of appropriate parties, generally representatives of affected groups, in decisions is essential. The more "voices" that provide information, the better subsequent decisions will be.

Also, definitions of goals, objectives, mission, and other components must be in measurable terms so it can be clearly seen whether or not those expectations were achieved. Moreover, feedback needs to be comprehensive and continuous. Continuous evaluation through this process will help the organization stay on track in terms of unity of purpose and action.

Budgeting: What It Is and What It Isn't

Budgeting has many definitions. In the school organizational context, budgeting at its simplest is a plan to manage resources. At its best, it is a plan for use of resources to accomplish organizational goals and to obtain maximum productivity. Productivity is the relationship between resources used by an organization and that organization's results, outputs, services value, and performance benefits ("bang for the buck"). School leadership calls for the following distinct parts:

- Identifying income and revenues from all sources well in advance of their intended use
- Evaluating current organizational status, standing, or performance through an appropriate assessment of needs
- Planning future expenditures and resource allocations in a way that will most likely produce the greatest achievement of organizational purpose
- Communicating the allocation plan appropriately within the social, political, and economic context in which the school organization dwells
- Providing smooth implementation for effective achievement of the purposes of the organization including use of sound fiscal and managerial control
- Evaluating the plan and allocations made for soundness, performance, and value derived and making changes as needed to provide for continuous improvement over time

School budgeting is part prediction, part communication, part planning, and part decision making. Decisions to be made are often very difficult, given the intricacy of school organizations and a pervasive public sensitivity for the gravity of educational consequences in modern-day society. Education is a high-priority component of modern life, and it provides the avenue for social, economic, and personal success and well-being. Education, in the minds of the public, provides a ticket to adult prosperity and happiness when coupled with ample effort and commitment. Its undertakings and activities often occupy the spotlight of public scrutiny and commentary, and its use of monies and other resources often is the center of the collective interest and focus of attention.

School-Based Budgeting

School-based budgeting is another way for school systems to make decisions and allocate resources. The process calls for individuals who implement budgetary decisions to help make those decisions. The idea is to put the power for making decisions at the organizational level closest to the decision. In school-based budgeting, the principal, in collaboration with staff and constituents, has been delegated the responsibility to budget resources at the individual building level. Given the discretionary authority to determine how resources are used in a given school, it's believed that people will feel a sense of ownership and commitment for improvement in the activities and programs within their school.

However, school-based budgeting, as with school-based management, in and of itself, is no guarantee of quality improvement. Several conditions have to be in place and some characteristics have to be prevented or eliminated. Regrettably, expected results of success have been inconsistent across the country (Mohrman & Wohlstetter, 1994).

Rationale for School-Based Budgeting

Given the challenge to improve schools, research has taught that efficiency and productivity are more likely to flourish with school autonomy than with extensive central control. In the use of resources, quality demands both central-ized and decentralized operations, but in different dimensions and with different responsibilities.

Centralization of authority has not always led to the outcomes that produc-tivity needs in schools. Educational history in recent decades has revealed that the central office has done some things well, and has done other things not so well. For example, central direction has been very effective in dealing with issues of jus-tice in equal access to educational opportunity. It has been less effective in dealing with issues of organization and operation of individual schools for instructional quality. Factors associated with effectiveness in instruction are more likely to be found at the individual school level (Barr & Tagg, 1995).

Another reason for school-based budgeting is simply that the school is fre-quently the basic cost center in the delivery of educational services. It is the small-est "whole" unit within the greater "whole" of the school system. Moreover, the principal is likely to be the most significant factor in the improvement of instruc-tion. Consequently, the belief is that the school system must be configured to allow individual schools to deal with their own problems, as much as makes sense. However, sufficient resources allocated from the system to deal with those prob-lems are essential for success.

There is a need for central direction and regulation and for the necessary forms of accountability. However, balance is needed that gives individual school units enough flexibility and discretion to effectively deliver their services and products. This balance of responsibility and distribution of authority should (1) foster prudent monitoring and sound execution of districtwide functions at the central level and (2) foster creative and ample autonomy for organizational deci-sion making aimed toward successful attainment goals and standards at the school level.

Central Responsibilities in School–Based Budgeting

There are shared and separate responsibilities in school-based budgeting, and the system needs to decide which is which. The governance team—superintendent and governing board—should have the responsibility to define and disseminate systemwide curriculum expectations and organizational goals. The overall system budget or spending plan must be established at the central level, although pru-dent judgment provides for broad and vertical organizational collaboration in the process.

Capital expenditures, including major maintenance and construction, are best planned and directed from the system level, as are other major systemwide activ-ities, such as energy management, food services, and transportation. Equity and standards in personnel selection generally also must be assured by the system office, including the screening of personnel and the administration of compensa-tion and benefits.

The board and superintendent must have major responsibilities in setting policies, developing and implementing regulations and procedures, defining staffing configurations and levels, and managing collective bargaining agreements.

In addition, textbooks and overall program tests and assessment procedures and instruments are best selected for districtwide use at the central level. Evaluation of performance against standards is perhaps the most important responsibility the board and superintendent have. Without careful assessment of results, no system has a way of knowing whether or not its expectations are being met.

School Responsibilities in School-Based Budgeting

It isn't enough that schools, or building-level administrators, receive increased autonomy and administrative discretion in decision making and organizational operations. In addition, any increase in authority must be always accompanied with an increase in accountability. School-based budgeting doesn't mean that schools have freedom to buy or spend anything they want. Rather, it means that schools have flexibility and greater latitude in decisions about how to allocate the resources designated for their school to best achieve success.

For example, one principal in a large Arizona suburban elementary school was allocated a certain number of teachers by the central office based upon the number of students in the school. The principal and people at that school mutually decided not to hire their full complement of teachers, but to use the salary monies of two teaching positions to hire paraprofessionals instead. They were able to hire three or four paraprofessionals to work with individual students for each teaching position they converted. The flip side was that all teachers had to accept a few more students in each classroom because of the resulting increases in class size. Further, the school was just as accountable for the results they received with their locally determined distribution of resources as before.

School-based budgeting also calls for collaborative planning, careful determination of strengths and weaknesses, clearly defined school goals and objectives, training and time to develop processes needed for implementation, and a monitoring system in place at the school level. In addition, different budget development procedures and processes are needed, which are explained later in this chapter.

Autonomy and discretion are two of the prime ingredients for leadership opportunity, and school-based budgeting provides a great setting for its development. You, as the administrator and leader, need to constantly seek new and better ways of doing things, with more cost-efficiency, to advance the quality of the learning environment under administrative direction. However, support and flexibility for significant school-level budget decisions are essential. Given these factors, school-based budgeting is another tool to help schools match available resources to the needs of their students, develop plans and programs to meet unique goals, and get the best results from efforts of the staff, faculty, and administration.

Systemwide Budgeting Processes

The basic purpose of a budget is to serve as a guide or plan for use of financial resources in the management of programs and services. The budget should

(1) provide a framework for the school system's work toward organizational goals within limited resources and (2) balance projected expenditures with anticipated revenues. It comes as no surprise to note that budget requests in most school systems generally exceed available financial resources. Of course, several approaches to budgeting are available to schools; but in this chapter, four levels or classifications of budgeting will be considered.

Levels of Budgeting

There are several kinds of budget processes, but all types fall into four classifications or levels. Formula, or administrative, budgeting is perhaps the most common in public schools. Less common is program budgeting and incremental budgeting. The least utilized budget process is performance-based, or sometimes called "curriculum-driven" budgeting (English, 1987).

Level 1: Formula (Line-Item) Budgeting

In formula budgeting, relationships between resources available and cost projections are established. Given a certain level of revenues, a configuration of services, materials, or other commodities is developed and organized in terms of its end use. In other words, its "object of expenditure" is the mode of organization such as salaries, benefits, supplies, purchased services, and so on. In effect the budget is a representation of what the system "buys," where it is used, and what it costs. The purchased or procured line item usually is not linked to the objective it ultimately addresses, and the connection is seldom defined in organizing projected costs.

In addition, the process is often "closely held," usually by a small policy-making or executive group or individual (superintendent or business official). The executive body reviews revenues and exercises control over the expenditures within defined procedures or formulas. Public or staff involvement in decision making is limited, and it is difficult to connect planned expenditures to specific educational objectives or purposes.

Level 2: Program Budgeting

In program budgeting, the purpose or intended activity of the expenditure is the organizing variable. This level involves organizing and presenting information about costs and benefits of the school's activities related to purposes or goals. Program budgeting establishes connections between programs, services, or activities with plans for allocation of funds. Objectives and goals are established, alternative programs are costed and considered, and allocations are made by choosing among the alternatives to the limit of available resources.

In program budgeting, it is possible to find tangible relationships between the school's programs and budget and to identify a planned (and observable) congruence between the purpose of the school and expenditures. Usually, the "function-object" classification of expense from level 1 is incorporated into level 2.

In effect, this type of budgeting makes it clear what the programs and activities of the system actually cost and what the money does, making it possible to compare costs and benefits more easily.

Level 3: Incremental Budgeting

Incremental budgeting is simply a process in which programs are organized into packages, or increments, costed separately, rank ordered as to preference, and funded in ordinal fashion up to the limit of available resources. "Zero-based" budgeting falls into this category. Incremental budgeting relies on a program structure, usually is convertible to object format, and involves decision making as to the level or quantity of service for a program. For example, class size could be treated as a program and funded at one of several increment levels, as shown in the following chart taken from a school district in Montana.

Incremental Budgeting: Class Size Example

Increment ID	Increment Name (w/Class Size)	Increment Cost	Cumulative Cost
101–01	Elementary instruction 1:30	$21,503,032	$21,503,032
101–02	Elementary instruction 1:28	$2,197,063	$23,700,095
101–03	Elementary instruction 1:26	$2,109,719	$25,809,814
101–04	Elementary instruction 1:24	$2,078,887	$27,888,701
101–05	Elementary instruction 1:22	$2,005,332	$29,894,033

In the above example, class size could be funded from 22 pupils per teacher to 30 pupils per teacher, depending upon how much the decision-making body determined to allocate for this program. It's interesting to note that in this district of about 25,000 pupils, increasing or reducing the average elementary class size by one pupil adds or subtracts about $1,000,000. This is just one way the process provides various decision options. In addition, other program packages (i.e., gifted and talented education, instrumental music, etc.) would be arranged in the same fashion, permitting funding at differential levels or with quantities of each program. In a sense, program increments compete for funding in this process.

Level 4: Performance-Based (Curriculum-Driven) Budgeting

Performance-based budgeting is often called curriculum-driven, data-driven, or results-based budgeting. The underlying nature of performance-based budgeting is to tie measured performance, or achievement of established outcomes or objectives, into the decision-making process. Funding is based upon the observable value obtained from the program and level. Resources are allocated by program activities, quantity or level, and measurements of results that link outcomes to resources. The aim is to implement a process that *results* in a planned budget based upon the measured and defined educational needs and accomplishments of a school system. Assessment data on educational effectiveness, or viability, is used to build the budget; and performance budgets are generally highly collaborative in nature and definitely lean toward decentralized decision making.

Over two decades ago, Fenwick English stated that "budget development and curriculum development should be intertwined, the latter preceding the former. The budget ought to be curriculum driven, when too often that is not the case" (English, 1987, p. 205).

Comparisons of Budgeting Levels

The four levels described previously are graphically illustrated in the proceeding exhibit. The exhibit shows how each level incorporates the features of the lower levels, and in a few words attempts to describe the nature of each level.

Budget Level Characteristics and Components

Characteristics and Components	Levels			
	I	II	III	IV
Formula/Object *(What is purchased)*	x	x	x	x
Purpose/Activity *(What is performed)*		x	x	x
Increment/Level *(What quantity is provided)*			x	x
Results/Performance *(What value is procured)*				x

Implementing School-Based Performance-Based Budgeting

School-based budgeting should provide for allocation of a school's discretionary funds based on assessment data and built with participation of key staff members. In this way, it can promote not only greater productivity but teamwork and commitment on the part of members of the organization as well. School-based budgeting uses the individual school's educational programs as the framework for planning and places the school's administrator right in the middle of the budgeting process. The specific configuration of the process depends upon many factors, particularly the capability of the system to define and measure quality and equity.

Quality can be measured in many different ways. For example, one school district evaluated the reading achievement levels of its elementary schools, finding considerable discrepancy and wide differences. The range of difference in one school system is shown in the chart below.

Mean Achievement Comparisons

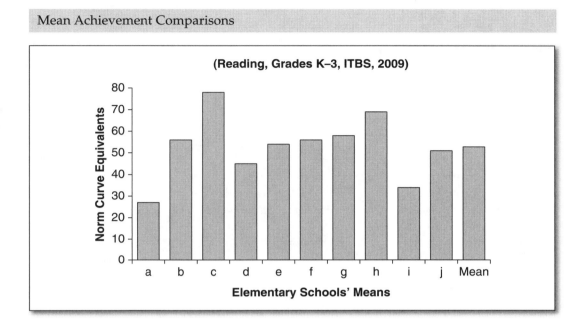

Introducing Equity in Budget Allocations

In the example above, reading achievement ranges from a norm curve equivalent score of 28 to a high of 83. Despite such discrepancy in achievement levels among schools, the school system had allocated staff resources uniformly to all of its schools for years. This resulted in each school receiving a formula allocation of one reading specialist for each 400 pupils. Since most elementary schools were about 900 students, each school received two specialists. After reviewing the assessment data, it was determined that allocation by enrollment was inequitable, and the assignment of reading specialists was changed. Specialists were assigned on the basis of measured pupil performance and differential needs in the reading program. Some schools received a part-time specialist; other schools received two or more specialists, depending upon distance from the district mean. Schools achieving below the mean received additional reading specialist time; schools above the mean received fewer services. This is one example of a performance-driven budget decision, and it is a manifestation of the principle of *equity*.

Equity is attending to individual differences in students and schools. Some schools achieve at lower levels than others, due mostly to the socioeconomic nature of the community and students. Providing equal resources to students with different needs perpetuates the discrepancies between groups; however, when allocations for programs, services, and materiél are structured in response to diagnosed needs, the "playing field is leveled." This is a very fundamental principle of commitment to individual needs and to assuring equal success among all clientele (learners).

> "There is nothing more unequal than the equal treatment of unequals."
>
> —Thomas Jefferson

Parents with two or more children know all too well that each child is unique and that uniqueness requires distinctive consideration and treatment. However, in schools, the "one size fits all" pattern often prevails, to the detriment of some individual learners.

Other Implementation Considerations

In performance-based budgeting, if guidelines and assigned responsibilities aren't properly worked out, problems can result. For example, one educational writer offered many proposals, some highly questionable, for school-based management. Among these were the suggestion that selection of textbooks be handled by individual schools and that reallocation of funds should be permitted within a school regardless of source.

Such reckless statements fail to recognize the inviolability of categorical funding (such as federally funded programs) or to acknowledge major standards of quality control in curriculum management within a school system. It wouldn't make sense to have several different textbooks at a given grade level in a school system, any more than it would make sense to have several different curricula. Another statement called for school principals to be accountable for energy costs within their school. This would cause shivers among principals of schools built before energy consciousness changed the way many schools were designed. Some common sense is called for in carefully delegating school responsibilities in budgeting.

Ignoring differential needs of individual schools will almost guarantee differential success.

GENERAL BUDGETING FACTORS

Several factors need to be considered in budgeting, and budgets must be prepared after a full examination and evaluation of each dimension. Factors to be considered include the following:

- Purpose and intended outcomes of each program (What does the program intend to accomplish?)
- Alternative activities and procedural options (What different ways can the outcomes be reached?)
- Personnel requirements: professional and support (What are the human resource requirements?)
- Matériel requirements: supplies and equipment (What are the things needed to do the job?)

- Space and environmental requirements (What conditions or facilities are required?)
- Assessment results from previous budget cycles (What do we know has worked before?)
- Cost projections for subsequent years (What cost alternatives are available?)
- Time requirements and scheduled flow of events (What are the reasonable time requirements?)

After information is obtained relative to the factors in budgeting, the planning process may begin. Certain assumptions then need to guide the planning, which are described in the next section.

Performance-Based Budgeting

Performance-based budgeting is uncommon in school systems in North America today. This process, referred to earlier as level 4 budgeting, requires the use of assessment data and evaluation information to determine whether or not, or to what level, a program receives funding. For example, if a drop out prevention program is funded for three years, the system is obligated to consider results of the program at some point. Given adequate performance, or success, the program may be considered for continued funding. If success is lacking, the program may need to be modified or terminated, releasing its funding for another intervention with greater promise.

In the vernacular, funded programs have to "put up or shut down" based on their results and success. Funding programs and services simply because they were funded in earlier years makes little sense if the results are known to be inadequate.

Performance-Based Budgeting Assumptions

Certain assumptions underlie budgeting for productivity. Focusing on the precepts of level 4 budgeting described previously, the budgeting process should be guided by the following assumptions:

1. Curriculum and instructional program outcomes can be defined.

2. Levels in achievement of programs may be identified and measured.

3. Results from assessment can be translated into program needs.

4. Needs and program priorities change over time.

5. Program needs can be expressed as budget requests.

6. Budget requests generally exceed available financial resources.

7. Assessment data and feedback can direct the establishment of priorities among programs.

8. Budget decisions should be driven by curriculum and program requirements and value.

An illustration of these assumptions was imbedded in comments of Glen Robinson, the former executive director of the Educational Research Service, when he stated,

> [T]he demand for improved educational productivity in our public schools lies at the heart of the educational reform and renewal movement. . . . The challenge to find ways of making schools more educationally effective, and at the same time more cost-efficient, could not have come at a more propitious time. . . . 20 years ago, there would have been little hard data and research on which to rely when making decisions (Robinson, 1986, p. 2).

Elements in Performance-Based Budgeting

As to how our process can be best implemented at the school level, several elements must be incorporated within curriculum-driven budgeting. These elements in the process include the following:

1. Budget requests should be built in incremental, programmatic form.
2. Principals and teachers must be active participants in the budget planning decisions.
3. Cost benefits of budget requests must be clearly delineated.
4. Priorities must be rank ordered by a school-based, decision-making body.
5. Requests publicly compete for funding priority.
6. Tangible evidence of program results must guide allocations.

Considering the above elements, it is easy to distill the performance budget into three basic characteristics, or hallmarks.

Hallmarks of a Performance-Based Budget

There are three hallmarks of a performance-based, or curriculum-driven, budget.

1. First, the developmental planning process preceding the budget must be participatory. That is, those who are affected by the budget decisions would be a part of the decision-making process. Submittal of requests and justifying needs is not enough. Unless teachers and principals, the primary deliverers of the mission, are involved in the actual budget decision-making process, the process cannot hope to be valid.

2. Second, the decision-making process must be public and open to scrutiny by others, especially parents and patrons. This calls for a format that is easily understood and well disseminated throughout the process. In the best of cases, even very large budgets can be presented in just a few pages in highly readable, comprehensive form, revealing ample program, financial, and performance information.

3. Third, budget ingredients should be comprised of increments, or connected pieces, of programs. These levels, or increments, can facilitate rank ordering on the basis of measured needs, demonstrated cost benefits, and assessment results. Increments build upon one another in cumulative fashion. This provides a tangible connection between what the money does and how much money is needed.

Given these three hallmarks, the performance budget process enables the system to be in a sound position to properly allocate funds or resources to carry out the system's needs and programs in priority order.

Moving Toward Performance-Based Budgeting

Once the school has put the system and tools together to link goals and performance feedback, it will be possible to move ahead with performance-based budgeting. Remember that it's critical for organizational goals, objectives, activities, and programs to be evaluated and reviewed on the basis of results *and* cost by a team of school personnel. Recommendations for budgeting must be independent of previous budget and program allocations and must not be recurrences of previous year formulas or decisions. Major steps for moving toward performance-based budgeting are delineated in the following section.

Developing Programmatic Units

Begin with identifying various educational activities or programs within the school, and group them into broad areas of like need, similarity of service, or commonality of purpose. Exclude all programs that are handled at other levels in the organization, such as textbook selection, utilities, transportation, and so on. An example might be "instruction—class size." Other examples might include "library services, student activities, custodial services, instrumental music, etc." Program units should be about twenty-five to forty in number. Having too many units complicates the decision process unnecessarily. More about this process will be discussed in later chapters.

Building Unit Increments

Within each programmatic unit, increments or "packages" are built, which provide varying levels of allocation (increasing or decreasing) from some standard. For example, last year's funding level may be used as a standard, and then several levels of funding can be developed above and below the standard. In this example, which is illustrated in the following table, if last year's budget provided library staffing sufficient to keep the library open four days a week, packages or increments could be built above or below that level and costed accordingly.

Program increments should be reasonable in number, but providing not more than five or six for each program unit is preferred for ease of management of the system.

Building Unit Increments Example

Increment Title	Description	Cost	Cumulative Cost
Library Services – Minimal	Professional staff provided two days per week at each school	$15,000	$15,000
Library Services – Current	Professional staff provided four days per week at each school	$15,000	$30,000
Library Services – Optimal	Professional staff provided five days per week at each school	$7,500	$37,500
Library Services – Augmented	Staff for small group and individual instruction at each school	$15,000	$52,500

Configuring Increment Packages

Each increment needs four things to be used in the budget process. First, each increment needs a goal statement or objective that defines what purpose it serves in measurable and operational terms. The goal or objective must be concise, easily understood, and able to deliver services if funded by itself. In other words, if funded at the increment's level, it must be able to stand alone and deliver a workable program or services within its cost allocation. Second, each increment must have a breakout and compilation of the delivery requirements to support the proposed activities, with full description and all accompanying costs. If the increment is class size, then teacher salaries, benefits, classroom quantities, and so on, are examples of things to be compiled and described. Third, each increment must have a defined cost, which describes what it will take to fund the increment independent of other increments. Last, each increment must have a report or digest of performance data if it has been operating previously or proposed strategies for measuring its accomplishment if newly developed. Organizational consequences, outcomes, or results should be clear from the evaluation data, whether the increment will or will not be funded.

Developing a Decision-Making Process

Guidelines and procedures for decision making must be established prior to implementation. The people who will be involved in the process should make recommendations as to how the process should proceed. Some guidelines used in other settings have included a number of useful items. For example, preparation of "catalog" type collections of program unit descriptions has been useful in keeping track of many different units and increments. Also, cost information in traditional line-item format has been useful for later conversion to standard budget reporting and accounting systems. Rules about assessment data have been helpful in narrowing down the breadth and scope of information that must be analyzed in detail later. In addition, the method by which units and increments will be rated and ranked by the decision-making body is a function that should be given considerable thought and definition beforehand.

Ranking Units and Increments

The most important task in the process is to rank order unit increments in priority order, based upon the democratic decision-making process and appropriate use of performance data. Descriptive information about the nature of a unit increment, its purpose and objective, its previous or proposed level of performance, and its cost are a few of the variables considered in the process. After increments are evaluated by the group and judged as to value or efficacy, they are ranked in order of preference. Several consensus-building processes are available for this purpose. An example of a ranking configuration, showing only an excerpt, is illustrated in the exhibit below.

Excerpt of Unit Increment Rankings

Rank	Unit-Increment Description	Cost	Cumulative Cost
67	Library media – collection expansion (1 book/student)	$14,123	$3,954,797
68	Guidance services – increase staff ratio to 1:325	$31,108	$3,985,905
69	Instrumental music – move start to Grade 4	$7,889	$3,993,794
70	Custodial service – schedule to 3 cleanings/week	$9,224	$4,003,018
71	Teacher assistance program – 2 hours/wk/teacher	$13,665	$4,016,683

Given the rank ordering described above, the system will have a tentative budget listing of unit increments in order of ranked priority.

Developing a Proposed Budget

Once the individual increments of the budget rank have been ordered, final development of the budget depends upon monies appropriated and higher-level reviews and decisions. The nice thing about the system is that available revenues might fluctuate up or down, but wherever the funding line is drawn, the increments to be included in the budget have been determined. If the revenues increase, more unit increment packages are funded. If revenues decrease, fewer unit increment packages are funded. In both cases, changes in monies available are dealt with in accordance with the predetermined priority order. In the preceding ranked table, if the school has $3,955,000 appropriated, package rank 67 is funded. If the school has $4,020,000 appropriated, then package rank 71 is funded, as are all packages with a higher ranking (but lower number).

Implementing and Evaluating the Budget

Within the budget system, both the process and the outcomes are monitored simultaneously. The allocation process must be scrutinized and improved over time. Also, the outcomes of the budget must be evaluated for future planning and budget decisions. Finances and programs must be analyzed and maintained or modified in accordance with their resultant levels of success. Given this approach to budgeting, you'll find that questions focus more on "How well are we doing?" rather than "How much did we spend last year?" Central management, the public, and the school team will have a more complete idea of what is (and what is not) funded in operations of the school. In addition, tangible linkages between program results, objectives, and costs will be apparent to all parties concerned. It will be far easier to explain why certain portions of the budget are increasing (or decreasing) from year to year.

Implementing the process usually requires three to four years of effort, with continuous revision of procedures and process based on findings and outcomes. See Appendix A for recommended actions typical of those proposed to school systems following curriculum management audits that do not meet the criteria for performance-based budgeting.

Organizational Benefits of Performance-Based Budgeting

Certain organizational advantages accrue to the school organization as a result of using curriculum-driven or performance-based budgeting. Some of the major benefits have been identified and are defined in the proceeding sections.

Credibility

A credible rationale is used for allocation of scarce resources. Limited economic, human, or matériel resources are brought into alignment with organizational goals on a rational basis. Organizational goals are funded in order of importance or perceived value in a reasonable, democratic process.

Feedback

Assessment feedback is used effectively in budget decisions. Objectives and results are brought into focus, relationships are used in planning, and measurement of efficacy is used in decision making.

Ownership

Participation in the budget planning and decision-making process by all members of the school team helps contribute to the acceptance of and commitment to final budget decisions. Such involvement undergirds and fosters corporate ownership of organizational processes and shared values.

Communication

Public visibility, team involvement, and an easy-to-understand format enable thorough public knowledge of district operations, goals, and program requirements. Such factors have often been associated with public trust and confidence in public schools.

Efficiency

Given competition for resources on a sound basis, efficiency improves. Duplication of effort is diminished, ineffective programs or strategies are terminated or modified, and low priority or unnecessary activities are eliminated.

Creativity

Creative thinking and problem solving are key parts of the budget process. Standard or traditional ways of doing things are subjected to scrutiny and evaluation; divergent thinking, which produces new and better ways of doing things, is also encouraged.

CONCLUSION

This chapter gives a brief overview of the complex performance-based budgeting process. It supports school-based management, which requires many effective tools to obtain productivity in school organizations. However, performance-based or curriculum-driven techniques offer new and powerful tools in the quest for productivity. They offer new tools to use on the complex and difficult management responsibility of budgeting. Of course, it requires willingness to function within certain procedures that may be significantly different than customary or traditional processes. However, given commitment to make performance-based budgeting work properly, school systems have found that this new paradigm:

- Leads to higher productivity,
- Fosters better organizational unity, and
- Holds promise for improved performance in school programs and activities.

The end result is that greater educational effectiveness with scarce or limited resources may be achieved. In times of financial paucity and economic difficulty, such new ideas and approaches to educational budgeting are welcome.

2

Why Change?

The Rationale for Performance-Based Budgeting

> Bernie Koch, vice president of the Wichita Chamber of Commerce, appeared before the Wichita (District No. 259) Board of Education to discuss the school system's newly implemented performance-based budget. Mr. Koch lamented that for several years there hadn't been a proposed school budget document of any depth that the public could examine, and he noted that it had been troubling for some time. The new performance-based budget was praised because the community was now able to "see and understand how their tax money was being spent" (Koch, 1995). According to Mr. Koch, the new approach was "a new building block to get us back to public confidence in the schools."

In public schools, there is never a shortage of critics and criticism. In point of fact, the annual Phi Delta Kappa Gallup Poll for 2009 reflects a history of the American public that indicates public schools are generally held to be inadequate, with less than 20% of poll respondents giving schools an A or a B in performance. Ironically, parents in the poll gave their own children's schools grades of an A or a B, with almost 75% awarding the high marks. Most Americans say that education is not as good as when they were in school; however, parents believe education is better today (Bushaw & McNee, 2009).

There is a hidden message with this dilemma of public confidence. Since parents are the most positive about the schools, and since parents are most likely to be the people in the community who visit the schools, it seems obvious that the more a person knows about an organization, the more supportive he or she may be. That certainly is the case with parents.

This is a not only a definable problem but a problem that can be solved, given appropriate attention to a plethora of issues, actions, conditions, and other matters. Key issues in finance center on transparency, integrity, and accountability. This chapter addresses a number of these problems and suggests some areas for consideration by school leaders.

FINANCIAL CHALLENGES FOR SCHOOL SYSTEMS

When it comes to budgeting in schools, the credibility picture becomes clouded. By a large margin, the majority of respondents nationally in the Phi Delta Kappa Gallup Poll for 2009 cited the lack of funding as the biggest problem facing schools. Parents cite lack of funding as their highest concern with schools as well. However, the lack of credibility in schools constitutes perhaps the single most important culprit in community resistance to financial support of public schools. The financial situation for schools today is reflected in a number of issues, including the following:

- The public believes that a major problem is the *lack* of funding for schools (Bushaw & McNee, 2009).
- Competition between public schools and alternative providers, such as private and charter schools, is increasing (Salisbury, 2003).
- School supportive population is dwindling—61% of homes have no children in school (Bushaw & McNee, 2009).
- Special needs are consuming a greater share of resources—special education cost has grown nearly four times as fast as regular education (Berman, Davis, Koufman-Frederick, & Urion, 2001).
- There is limited support for addressing the achievement gap, largely predicted by socioeconomic factors beyond the control of the school (English & Steffy, 2001).

Despite the increase in expenditures for public education, the image of education in terms of sufficient funding to achieve a suitable and acceptable level of performance remains in jeopardy. In actuality, public schools' enrollment and expenditures have both grown over time, as shown in the subsequent chart.

In this chart, both the enrollment and the expenditures per student grew over this eleven-year period, even with the dollars controlled to reflect actual cost with 2006–2007 dollars (National Center for Educational Statistics, 2009). With financial needs growing because of an expanding pupil population, the relationship between public confidence and school district expenditures is critical. Economic confidence is the catalyst for adequate financial support for schools.

Enrollment and Expenditures per Student 1995–2006

Year	Enrollment	Expenditure* per Student
1995–96	44,840,000	7,515
1996–97	45,611,000	7,608
1997–98	46,127,000	7,810
1998–99	46,539,000	8,072
1999–2000	46,857,000	8,333
2000–01	47,204,000	8,604
2001–02	47,672,000	8,853
2002–03	48,183,000	9,016
2003–04	48,540,000	9,114
2004–05	48,795,000	9,275
2005–06	49,113,000	9,390

*Constant 2006–07 dollars

BUILDING ECONOMIC CONFIDENCE

Educational organizations need to demonstrate more than financial needs to obtain adequate funding—they need to recognize, implement, and demonstrate three components of economic confidence which were conceptualized by Marvin Pomerantz, former president of the Iowa Board of Regents (Pomerantz, 1995). The components of economic confidence include the following:

- *Prudence*. demonstrating efficiency and integrity in the use of publicly supplied financial and operational resources
- *Alignment*. living within the means available to the system—adjusting budget levels to match revenue levels
- *Performance*. connecting system priorities to results and showing gains in productivity

This three-dimensional relationship of the components of economic confidence can be expressed graphically as shown in the following illustration (Pomerantz, 1995).

Pomerantz observed that the public no longer supports or is enthusiastic about funding public institutions without accountability for the three components above.

Economic confidence starts with the premise that public institutions, particularly schools, first have to show that funding received in the past has been used wisely and prudently. If perceptions of previous financial stewardship are flawed,

Components of Economic Confidence in Public Educational Institutions

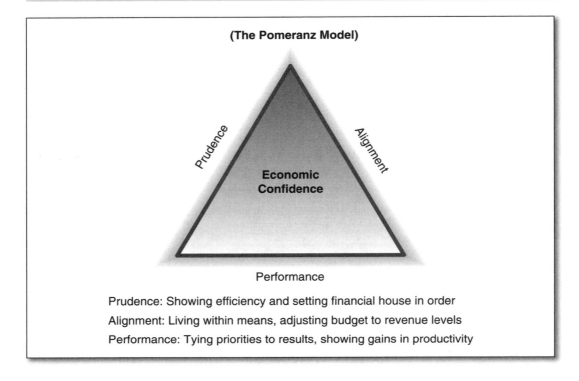

(The Pomeranz Model)

Prudence

Alignment

Economic Confidence

Performance

Prudence: Showing efficiency and setting financial house in order

Alignment: Living within means, adjusting budget to revenue levels

Performance: Tying priorities to results, showing gains in productivity

public confidence is eroded. For example, if a public official wrongly uses public resources for personal benefit, and this becomes known, the public support will be jeopardized.

At the same time, alignment of spending within resources available is also critical. Overspending and/or underspending an authorized funding level is perceived by the public as irresponsible and indicative of faulty management. Living within the organization's means is commonly an expectation for public institutions. If budgetary limits are not honored, the perception is that the organization is not in control of itself.

The most important factor seen in this model of economic confidence is that of performance. Once funds are acquired, the public needs to see that their support was well utilized and results of the funding were reasonable and adequate in terms of what was accomplished. However, if results are inadequate or unsatisfactory, public perceptions are diminished accordingly.

Ironically, public confidence in public schools has suffered in recent decades, perhaps beginning with *Why Johnny Can't Read* by Rudolf Flesch, 1955, and continuing to recent years (Bracey, 2008). The theme that "schools are awful" is not without its adherents across the United States today. The uphill struggle to obtain public confidence in public institutions in general and schools in particular begins with addressing factors of economic confidence.

Factors of Inadequacy and Ineffectiveness in School System Budgeting

There are several things lacking in many public school systems when it comes to adequate and effective budgeting practices. Findings in curriculum management audits conducted in the past two decades indicate the following practices are faulty in school systems with respect to budgeting (Poston & Anton, 2005):

- System budget policy fails to spell out how and why budgeting will take place, and budgeting usually is a function of the current administrative authority in power, which may result in politicized budget allocations.
- Participation in the budgeting process is frequently limited to a select few individuals, which limits information, perspective, and effective decision making.
- Allocations are not in accordance with measured needs of clientele or connected to system goals, creating inequity and a lack of constancy of purpose.
- Internal and external publics have limited, often distorted, information about the system's budget and financial affairs, and cost-benefit analyses are seldom employed in budgeting.
- Feedback information about pupil achievement factors and system performance is flimsy, making accurate judgments about the efficacy of programs and services virtually impracticable.

The factors undermining effectiveness in school system budgeting are exacerbated by problems typically experienced by systems in their existing budgeting process. Some of the more common problems in budgeting are drawn for school system experience (Poston, 2009).

Typical Problems Noted in School System Budgeting

In school system budgeting, many problems occur that are frequently not under control of the system. Many agencies impose rules or strictures that constrain and delimit system discretion and capabilities. Some of the more common issues and problems include the following.

- *Forecasting revenues.* In many states and provinces, the finalization of financial allocations to systems is often delayed, making revenue projections difficult and unpredictable.
- *Unfunded external mandates.* Legislative mandates frequently affect school systems' operating costs, but funding from the external agency is regularly inadequate or omitted altogether. For example, special education mandates provide insufficient funding for implementation, causing other system resources to be diverted to subsidize the mandated program.
- *Balancing inflation against program costs.* It is often the case that factors affecting costs, such as salary obligations, benefits increases, and similar unforeseen demands exceed revenue growth rates which may be based upon inflationary trends, creating stress from overextended resources.

- *Public confidence and support.* Augmentation of system funding is possible in many states and provinces, subject to the approval of voters in a tax or budget referendum. Referenda for additional funding for educational purposes have not shown high approval rates. In Wisconsin, budget increase referenda averaged only 40.1% approval over a decade, and were even worse—35.1%—when coupled with bonding requests (Maher & Skidmore, 2007).
- *Information for decision making.* One of the vexations in school system budgeting has always been access to and understanding of massive amounts of complicated data. School officials are not normally trained in accounting, and data are occasionally formulated in detailed diminutive form, making a conceptual grasp implausible.
- *Unexpected events/shortfalls.* Infrequently, unexpected events occur which affect funding availability for school systems. For example, in Iowa in 2009, the governor mandated without discussion that all school systems in the state reduce their budgets with an across-the-board cut of 10% three months after the school year had begun (Jacobs, 2009). Such a dramatic political move created two problems in budgeting for school systems—an urgent need to find alternative sources of funding to meet obligations and a corresponding reduction in cash reserves, which in turn increased short term debt to meet obligations.
- *"Bomb bigger than plane."* This phenomenon was attributed to a society that makes demands so immense for schools that the school systems are rendered helpless to respond because the system can't handle all the tasks it is asked to perform. In this metaphor, the bomb is the sum total of the missions laid upon the school system, which is the plane (English & Steffy, 2001).

After reviewing many of the deficiencies, problems, and shortcomings that stimulate systems to consider changing or modifying attributes and processes of budgeting, the gap between where systems are and where they need to be is substantial. In view of that, some needs currently not adequately being met are in need of change or modification. A few of those needed changes are discussed in the following sections.

The Need for Cost-Benefit Analyses in School Systems

Given the current state of local school systems' budgeting practices, it is very difficult, if not impossible, to organize data and implement procedures that provide linkages between the allocation of resources and the specific, differential needs of clientele. Regrettably, the use of cost analysis in decisions about resource allocation has been less than adequate. Assessing costs in light of measured effectiveness or productivity is a highly uncommon practice in school systems.

Studies of the impact of money upon school effectiveness have been mixed, and establishing a connection between funds spent on education and specific student achievement results has proven difficult and controversial (Hummel-Rossi & Ashdown, 2002). However, it is widely believed that simply increasing the amount of money allocated to education will not necessarily result in improved student achievement or the effectiveness of the school organization. Sound budgeting practice requires a businesslike approach to fiscal allocations that goes beyond what the funds will purchase or provide. Any public school system needs to provide more complete information on the relationship between planned expenditures and the nature of the outcomes that are anticipated to be realized by the program or service being funded. Regrettably, the amount and quality of existing cost-effectiveness endeavors have been questionable in the past (Levin & McEwan, 2002).

Cost-benefit analysis requires a delineation of outcomes of a measureable educational alternative (program, service, support mechanism, tools, etc.), which then can be directly compared to its monetary costs. This ultimately places a value on the particular outcome, thereby permitting the system to determine whether benefits planned or received are worth the cost or are desirable. Comparisons may be drawn across a wide spectrum of educational alternatives, enabling the decision-making group or individual to make choices that allocate resources to more effective or appropriate interventions or end uses.

Of course, the simplest form of cost-benefit analysis requires a clear definition of the goals and objectives of a specific activity, intervention, or endeavor; a comprehensive compilation of every resource needed in the activity; and a thorough compilation of the activity's costs. That information identifies what the activity is actually expected to return and at what cost. The determined value is then useful in decision-making processes.

In performance-based budgeting, cost-benefit analysis is imbedded in all levels of budgeting above the line-item type of budget (program/activity, incremental, and results-based); however, most school systems use only the "level 1" budgeting approach, which thwarts value determinations of cost-effectiveness. Usually, the budgeting process is built piece by piece of individual line items, such as salaries, benefits, materials, utilities, and so on, which hinders a detailed understanding of values and outcomes. A comprehensive knowledge of results and relationships to costs is provided only at the program/activity level (level 2) or higher.

The Case for Participatory Decision Making

Despite the universal mission of school systems, decision making is usually based on a series of qualitative and quantitative data related to physical conditions and trends. The collection of information is often comprehensive; however, decisions are frequently made without broad participation of the various parties in the school system and its community.

Lessons learned from successful decision making in school systems imply that decision-making processes have to be participatory. Cooperation has to supplant competition (Deming, 1993). Learning is most successful in a highly supportive environment, in which students, teachers, parents, and community members work closely and harmoniously together.

Some of the key benefits of participatory decision making include the following:

- *Transparency.* Information, priorities, strategies, financial standing, and actions are open to all stakeholders either directly or through representation.
- *Ownership.* Fidelity to decisions in which stakeholders have participated is enhanced.
- *Quality.* Better decisions result from broader involvement of diverse populations, which is one of the underlying features of democratic governance.
- *Equity.* Groups that are usually included in the decision-making process have more opportunity to present their concerns and defend their interests.
- *Accountability.* By sharing in decision making, stakeholders are accountable in accordance with the tasks to which they have committed themselves.
- *Efficiency.* Shared information and decisions taken in common avoids misunderstandings, duplication of effort, and contradictory opposition.

Taking all these reasons into account, it is clear that participatory decision making is an attribute of sound governance and supports institutionalization of decisions due to cooperation and linkages between stakeholder groups.

The Essentiality of Feedback and Assessment in Budgeting

It goes without saying that the better information one has to make a decision, the better the decision will be. Correspondingly, decisions made with accurate and complete information beforehand have a greater likelihood to be sound and appropriate under those circumstances.

Unfortunately, assessment information is often inadequate in school systems, and use of what assessment information there is in decision making is often ineffective. The question becomes, "What will it take to have adequate assessment information in budgeting so as to gain effective decision making?" To answer the question, one may look to the curriculum management auditing standards, which provide a clear and comprehensive idea of what is expected in school systems (Frase, English, & Poston, 2000).

In the curriculum management audit model, relevant criteria call for assessment practices that are

- keyed to a valid, officially adopted, and comprehensive set of goals/ objectives of the school system;
- used by the policymaking groups in the system and the community to engage in specific policy review for validity;
- used to establish costs and select needed curriculum alternatives; and
- publicly reported on a regular basis in terms that are understood by key stakeholders in the community.

Moreover, some additional expectations relevant to budgeting processes include:

- Use of a student and program assessment plan that provides for diverse assessment for varied purposes at all levels—system, school, and classroom

- A timely and relevant base of data upon which to analyze important trends in student achievement
- A vehicle to examine how well specific programs and activities are actually producing desired learner outcomes or results
- A database to compare the strengths and weaknesses of various programs and program alternatives, as well as to engage in equity analysis
- A database to modify or terminate ineffective educational programs
- A method/means to support a programmatic budget and enable the school system to engage in cost-benefit analysis

The curriculum management audit criteria here describe several traits of an effective school system. First, the criteria stipulate that the organization has goals and objectives—in effect, the organization has defined purposes and expectations. These aspirations or intentions provide the marks of effectiveness in organizational operations and functions. Private sector literature is replete with the necessity of established organizational direction, a key requisite for constancy of purpose (Deming, 1986).

People in any organization simply need to know the nature of the business with which the organization is involved. In essence, what is the organization's intended purpose? Educational organizations are established to design and deliver learning, among other things; without goals and objectives delineating organizational direction, however, the school system's people and operations could become unfocused and disconnected.

Second, the audit criteria call for ways and means to effectively measure or assess how the organization is doing against its goals and objectives. It further calls for a database to determine the efficacy of programs, interventions, equity, and production of student learning—the main thing. Without such a comprehensive and relevant database, the system is unable to determine if it is succeeding in accomplishing its stated mission. With such a database and system, the organization becomes enabled to measure its progress, modify its activities, and make changes in the organization based on valid, dependable information.

Finally, the criteria call for a method or means to support programmatic budgeting and enable the school system to engage in cost-benefit analysis. Programmatic budgeting structures expenditures within defined objective-based activities or programs, with expenditure objects encased within. In effect, program budgeting plans expenses within a body of work, including underlying objectives of the body of work, activity, or program, and including all related expenses (units, staff, matériel, etc.), the combination of which is then treated as a stand-alone entity.

Program budgeting places the emphasis on what the money does, not so much what the money is or what it is for in terms of end use (purchases, payroll, etc.). Systems that move to programmatic budgeting find that the program entity has a defined, easily identifiable overall cost (as opposed to a long compilation of unrelated expense items), making it much easier to evaluate the activity's worth or value. It is the starting point for accountability for results in budgeting and cost-benefit analysis.

In summing up, the assessment system provides information for decision making (feedback) in budgeting based on goal accomplishment and worth of results. No school system can get better or more productive in reaching its goals without a comprehensive, valid, and rigorous assessment system.

Summary: Rationale for Change in Budgeting

This chapter has explored six faces of the challenge facing school systems in terms of (1) meeting financial challenges in funding and implementing effective organizational work to provide quality learning; (2) building economic confidence elements and actions needed to obtain alignment, prudence, and performance; (3) facing inadequacy and ineffectiveness in school system budgeting, including resolving problems and issues; (4) recognizing the need for cost-benefit analysis; (5) unleashing the power of participatory decision making; and (6) developing and using sound procedures in assessment to drive budgeting decision making.

With (1) perseverance and commitment to these standards, (2) the school system's focus on desired ends, (3) congruent operational implementation of the work, and (4) effective monitoring of feedback and results, the organization's growth in productivity will be greatly enhanced.

OPTIONAL ACTIVITY: ASSESSING STATUS OF BUDGETING PRACTICES

To determine how a given system measures up to this challenge and to identify needs or gaps between current status and desired status, an optional assessment instrument has been developed. It is provided in Appendix B at the back of the book.

Scoring: To score this instrument, simply allocate the following points:

+2 points for strongly agree

+1 point for agree

0 points for no opinion

−1 point for disagree

−2 points for strongly disagree

Note: Items numbered 2 and 19 are scored in reverse (−2 points for strongly agree, −1 point for agree, +1 point for disagree, and +2 points for strongly disagree).

Score Interpretation: An average group composite score of more than +20 points indicates that most of the criteria are followed, standards are met, and the system is working to implement programmatic budgeting. Of course, an average score of lower than 20 points for a group indicates that the system falls short in its capabilities to achieve effectiveness, transparency, and accountability in budgeting processes. Basically, a change in budgeting processes is needed for improved productivity.

Budget Planning for Financial Effectiveness and Efficiency

Schools have always felt the squeeze of doing more with less. In California, despite record population growth and changes in clientele, financial support historically has been in jeopardy. John Dean, superintendent of Orange County schools, pointed out that the "burden on school systems already stretched" continued to grow. Rudy Castruita, superintendent of Santa Ana schools, bemoaned the financial predicament—"we tried our best to stay out of classrooms (for cuts) . . . (but now) we have to do it again. There's even less to work with. We have to do more with less again" (Eng, 1991). The thrust for efficiency in school budgets never subsides.

Budgeting resources for use in a school system setting requires careful planning using the best information possible about a school system's operational and organizational status and quality. Planning with comprehensive and informative facts and figures enables the system to steer organizational decision making about allocations, desirability of programs or services, and ways and means for improving productivity to get the greatest benefit from the least expense.

School budgeting is at best an inexact science and a complex art. There is no easy way to provide "adequate" resources in budgeting for public school systems, given the constraints and complexities of educational organizations. Budgeting is partially built upon a foundation of uncertainty for the school organization, since budget activities and operations are constantly changing, the supply of resources is continually fluctuating, and the system's clientele is characterized by ongoing variability and emerging and unmet needs.

Budget planning involves many skills, a great deal of knowledge, and managerial diligence in order to be an effective tool for the educational leader. However, school finance is sometimes perplexing to non-financial educational leaders, and the job of budgeting is not easy given its nature. Effective and successful educational leaders must master the technology of budget planning and use it as a tool for achievement of the educational organization's purpose.

ELEMENTS OF EFFECTIVE BUDGET PLANNING

To begin with, some distinctions need to be clarified about the difference between a "plan" and "planning." In educational organizations, plans are often developed for a variety of reasons, including compliance with an external agency or authority, responses to changing circumstances, or other reasons. Effective planning doesn't necessarily focus on a document or identifying a strategy as a consequence of planning; rather, it focuses on analysis of information and synthesis of meaning for choosing courses of action (Mintzberg, 1994).

Planning efforts within a school system accomplish a number of things. For example, planning activities

- provide a strategic vision for where the system is headed;
- use available data projections for the future;
- incorporate long-term budget implications; and
- guide and inform the development of plans at all levels within the organization (Downey, Steffy, Poston, & English, 2009).

Planning is far more than a document, which may or may not guide the actions of the educational organization. The power and usefulness of planning emerges when it is a fluid, active, and dynamic process, which conceptualizes a vision for what can be and provides blueprints for results-oriented progress (Kaufman, Herman, & Watters, 1996).

School organizations that are not looking ahead five or more years, that are not paying attention to anticipated changes and forces, and that are not responding accordingly will find themselves in a reactive rather than a proactive mode. With those unwelcome circumstances, the system can expect to experience unnecessary complexity, distasteful dissonance, and undue turbulence in endeavors toward its mission.

Components of an Effective Budget Plan

Budgeting processes are characterized by a number of elements, or components. The effective budget plan contains at least six or seven distinct and separate components that are built upon sound organizational principles and well-established "best practice." The steps include establishment of purpose, planning operations, needs assessment, prediction and justification of estimates, governance judgment or consensus and approval, and plan implementation and evaluation.

Establishment of Purpose

Rational organizations moving toward congruence and achievement are characterized by well-defined purposes (Deming, 1986). The rational school system has a defined and functional mission, objectives, and strategies to accomplish its purpose. The mission states and clarifies for all stakeholders the primary values of the organization and fosters common commitment toward a central purpose over the long term.

Of course, establishing what the system seeks to achieve provides a very important focus for any organization. In educational organizations, the main point is effective delivery of learning for all clientele, and accomplishment of that purpose needs to clearly drive decisions and choices. To be performance-based, results of efforts and decisions need to be evaluated in terms of accomplishment of the organizational purposes.

Objectives are shorter-term aims congruent with the organizational purpose and mission. Strategies define things or activities to be done and how to do them and include assignment of responsibilities, cost information, and time elements. Without a specific list of activities, planned costs, and timetables, the organizational direction can be fragmentary, contradictory, and incongruent with organizational purpose. Also, it is difficult to measure the effectiveness of ill-defined activities and organizational actions.

Planning Operations

Planning operations are enhanced when they keep focused on organizational goals and the people involved in the process are well-organized and efficient in planning processes. Policy constraints affect allocations, establish priorities, and aid in the establishment of a "game plan" or blueprint for action.

Some of the operations the organization needs to place into action include the following:

- *Policy expectations.* Governing boards need to place into policy clear expectations for the system's leadership, staff, and patrons. These expectations include thinking collectively about the future in tangible form based upon valid information.
- *Leadership vision.* Leadership needs to have an implicit and an explicit idea of the general direction of where the system is heading in terms of improvement of organizational operations and results. Sometimes, this is thinking about what the organization needs to be doing compared to what it is currently doing to determine discrepancies, which can be expressed as needs of the system.

In times of financial stress, which confront school systems from time to time, new thinking about school budgeting is needed. The current financial situation demands linkage between the educational effectiveness of the school system with cutting-edge procedures and processes for allocating limited resources toward school goals. In the past, little attention has been given to school productivity and even less consideration has been given to connections between educational outcomes and the distribution of resources. The hope is to change that with a performance-based budgeting system (PBBS).

Budgeting must be built upon the educational values of the school system. Performance-based budgeting applies the best that other budgeting processes have to offer, most specifically from the program and incremental types, and then some. Performance-based budgeting offers a way to link effectiveness of the basic mission of the school system to costs, and then to use that information in participatory decision making for developing a budget.

The challenge is to show tangible, visible, and logical relationships between curricular (teaching and learning) needs and financial priorities. Basically, the system needs to put its money where its mission is, and performance-based budgeting offers one way to do just that.

Over the last eight years, the state legislature has increased formula funding a total of 6.1%, or about ¾ % per year. However, during that same period of time, the consumer price index has risen 19.1% or about 2.3% per year. Due to this inadequate funding support, the system has to implement a budget adjustment (reversion) process for the coming fiscal year. While this is always a difficult process, the PBBS will provide a way to emphasize system goals and priorities in these budget decisions.

The purpose of performance-based budgeting is to distribute scarce resources across school needs and priorities based upon shared values. Performance-based budgeting processes relate what is requested in a budget with what is needed to gain productivity. The vehicle to get it done is a value-based decision-making process laced with consensus techniques which results in programmatic priorities. For the system, the advantages of the performance-based budgeting system are

- Cost benefit analysis of resource allocations can provide guidance for priorities set forth in the strategic plan.
- District priorities and goals will be reflected in resource allocations, enabling recovery and reallocation of resources for continued improvement.
- The participatory process of PBBS is consistent with our goal and model of shared decision making.
- PBBS provides a workable and effective process for establishing the budget in either growth or retrenchment modes.

- *Valid information.* Budget planning needs to be informed and based upon valid and unequivocal data. Too often school organizations use data that are closer to speculation or anecdotal opinion. Solid evaluative information helps buttress decision-making processes in budgeting.
- *Connectivity.* Budgets are actually planning documents, so it stands to reason that budget planning needs to operate within the overall system planning process and to be connected in a congruent manner with system and unit planning direction.

Needs Assessment

Educational leaders can never have enough information. If they had perfect information, they would make perfect decisions. In effect, this means that the better the information, the better the decisions will be. The needs assessment component is for the sole purpose of obtaining legitimate and complete information about where the organization currently is and how that is different from where the organization wants or wishes to be.

Other aspects are also helpful, including diagnoses of demands upon the organization, defined performance levels and organizational characteristics, cost experience data, and effects of previous activity. These data are useful in analyzing organizational needs and projecting possible resource allocation decisions based upon a framework of robust information.

Prediction and Justification of Estimates

Prediction is the art of estimating future performance or activity based on previous history or past experience. It stands to reason that budget predictions are best drawn from budget history and measures of performance. Remarkably, many school budgets are simply based upon previous years' allocations, not expenditures or results.

The amount of expenditure required for current practices or activities is a more reliable measure of future cost than allocations. Plans built upon plans ignore the benefits of experience and assessment of performance. The use of performance data is critical in determining the efficacy or value of previous expenditures for any organization and is best used to augment actual cost information itself. The chart on the following page is an example of one school system's device for tracking previous expenditures and performance compared with budgeted amounts.

With similar information gathered, tabulated, and analyzed, school leaders can get an accurate understanding of how allocations and actual expenditures match up. With this information, better judgment can be exercised in determining actual needs of school units. It is important to remember that use of this information is also helpful in determining if individual subunits of the system are making effective use of resources.

If resources are delegated to individual schools, patterns of expenditures can be useful for monitoring program or activity history. Shortfalls, overallocations,

Budget Planning Worksheet for Budget Period: _____

A	B	C	D	E	F	G	H
Line Item (Object)	Current Year Expenditure	Current Year Budget	Variance (B-C)	Next Year Projected	Next Year Budget	Variance (B/F=%)	Assessment Data Summary and Reference Sources

system efficacy, and operational conflicts can be identified if the cost history includes measures of actual performance. Performance data provide the "proof of the pudding" and indicate how well the system's activities are reaching their intended goals or purposes.

Governance Consensus and Approval

School organizations are most commonly governed by a legislative and magisterial board, usually elected and usually comprised of laypersons. The body, or board, frequently has legislated authority to approve budget allocation recommendations from the employed professional staff. Such approval is predicated upon an understanding of the system needs, direction, requirements, priorities, assumptions, and measured performance. The board as a rule has both a policy and oversight function, and budget information must be sufficient to help the board adequately discharge both sets of responsibilities. The specific role of the board should not infringe upon executive duties or responsibilities (Poston, 1994) in building and recommending budgets.

Board involvement in management processes, including budget development and formation, may create organizational problems, including

- *Diminished administrative accountability.* If the board makes administrative decisions, the administration may not be held accountable for the consequences.
- *Loss of independence and interjection of bias.* When the board is involved in committees and development of recommendations to the whole board, it is in effect giving itself advice—which may or may not be objective and valid.
- *Politicization of direction.* Board members may skew the direction of the organization in an unbalanced or political manner.
- *Distortion of perspective.* Proactive board involvement in management operations may impair conceptual judgment because of an immersed point of view.
- *Abatement of integrity.* Perceived self-interest may undermine confidence and mutual respect.
- *Chilling effects on candor and honesty.* It is eminently more difficult for school system employees to confront openly and honestly the ideas and opinions of board members.

Organizational effectiveness is better served when board member roles and responsibilities are focused on key governance functions, such as policy determinations and system oversight. Legal adoption of the system budget is generally assigned to the governing board, as well, within most states and provinces.

Budget Plan Implementation and Evaluation

Implementing the budget, or carrying out its intent, is not the final step. There is no way for the organization to improve the quality of its performance over time unless it obtains feedback information. Evaluation is an essential phase of implementation, and data gathered are used during implementation activities to guide actions and decisions. Evaluation after implementation summarizes progress made, or the lack of progress, toward organizational goals and purposes.

Implementation involves commencing the work of the organization within the resource configuration and activities authorized and funded within the budget plan. The budget acknowledges a certain level of revenues and income for the system. The budget also authorizes expenditures for salaries, supplies, support, equipment, and other items for organizational work. How those authorizations are organized is an important part of the budget process. Authorized revenues and expenditures may be organized by line item, program or service area, incremental levels, or priority based upon worth and value of program components.

Implementation of budget plans often involves delegation of authority and, in recent years, delegation to individual subcomponents within the organization. Decentralization of authority within budget limits or parameters has many names, including site-based management, local school empowerment, high-involvement organization, school-based management, and similar designations. Decentralization is discussed in Chapter 7.

In the implementation phase, the budget is a plan—that is, it is a guide to discretionary action. As one pundit exclaimed, "the budget is a game plan, not a traffic cop." The budget provides a tool to management with financial and other resource options and alternatives, and implementation requires attention to and compliance with budget limitations. However, as will be seen later, some elements of flexibility in implementation are essential for quality improvement (Frase, English, & Poston, 2000).

Functions of the Budget

The performance-based budget is a "living" document, and it builds capability to serve a variety of functions, including the following:

- *Fosters activity of the organization toward long-term goals.* This function facilitates development and consistency of the organization's focus and purpose.
- *Guides decision making and leaders in carrying out activities.* Decision making does not occur in a vacuum, and a budget document provides direction and constraints for leadership decisions.
- *Enables choices on the potential, use, and worth of resources.* Many activity or program goals may be achieved in numerous ways, some better than others—the budget is the arena for such choices.
- *Provides a monitoring tool for cost-benefit relationships.* This function enables the organizational leadership to evaluate ongoing progress toward goals within financial constraints.
- *Promotes efficiency and productivity.* Collaborative planning and evaluation of options stimulates organizational thinking and activities to move toward maximizing results within available resources.
- *Links management and action.* Budget documents identify and specify management responsibilities in pragmatic ways and means for viable management endeavors.

- *Identifies the return on investment.* The performance-based budget process unambiguously links what is to be achieved and the scope of its cost.
- *Permits and motivates management to control costs and to achieve organizational goals.* No educational organization has unlimited resources, and efficiency and discriminating judgment are needed accordingly.
- *Connects intentions, experience, performance, and resource use.* The connectivity and coordination of the organization are more coherent when these variables are included in the evaluative process for budget allocations.

The budget plan has many functions and uses, but primarily, the budget is a tool for quality improvement and control. Control in the budget sense tilts toward "discipline" in meaning, indicating that the organization is in control of itself. Linking the goals of the organization with its activities, budgeted resources, and evaluation efforts is an example of quality control. Quality improvement has been described by Deming (1986) and others, and is figuratively characterized by the following diagram:

Illustration of Quality Improvement Components

Quality improvement for organizations involves the basic components of system thinking: clear and valid aims and purposes, effective and team-oriented actions and activities, and continuous assessment for feedback of leadership. The three prongs of quality improvement assure the organization of greater likelihood of constancy of purpose, congruent work aligned with purposes, and feedback about performance for use in additional planning and decision making for improvement (English, 1986).

Performance-based budgeting fits into the quality improvement cycle in a couple of ways. First, it provides the resources necessary to effectively carry out the work, which is defined in objective terms; it describes the functions and activities to be supported; and it requires budgeting decisions to be grounded in feedback data about results. "Closing the loop" assures the best use of resources for organizational activities and alignment with organizational purposes.

Budgeting as a Part of Long-Range Planning

Organizational planning is a very useful function to muster widespread support, commitment, and ownership of organizational goals, to develop potent actions and team synergy, and to monitor how well the system is responding and progressing against its needs.

Budgeting incorrectly often precedes goal development and activity determinations. However, that is not unlike the proverbial "cart before the horse." In school organizations, the budget frequently drives the curriculum, when it ought to be the other way around. As shown in the illustration which follows, budgeting is a natural and useful part of the planning process.

Relationships Between Goal Setting, Budgeting, and Evaluation in Planning

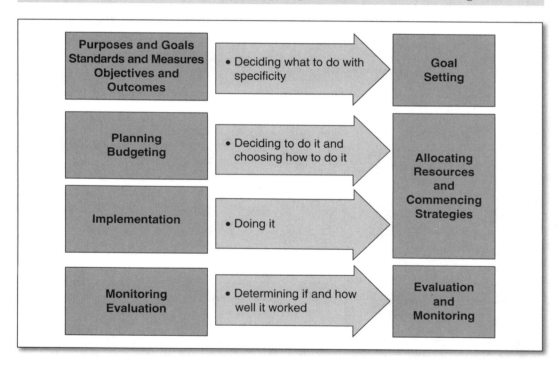

Planning processes, by definition, involve the determination and assignment of resources. Where budgeting fits in the process and what role or weight it provides in decision making is the key to administrative effectiveness.

Given the complexities of educational organizations, the uncertainty of resources and demands, and the close scrutiny of the public, school budgeting is not an easy job. School budgets mirror school organizations—they are labor intensive, nonprofit in design, and service and client oriented. Some school systems operate with as little as a small amount of dollars for each student, frequently face stagnant or declining resources, and find choices to be made more and more difficult over time.

The range of available financial resources varies widely across the United States school systems. In 2006, school systems in the United States spent an average of about $9,400 per pupil per year. Amazingly, some districts spent nearly half that—Utah spent about $5,600—and others spent a great deal more—New Jersey spent about $15,400 (U.S. Department of Education, 2008).

Some school districts have minimal control over the amount of their revenues, while others have a great deal of control over revenues; but how those resources are used is a key part of the philosophy underlying performance-based budget planning.

THE PARABLE OF THE TAILOR'S CLOTH

To determine the quality of planning in concert with budgeting, it's important to consider the direction of the planning process. As discussed earlier, goal setting and planning need to precede budget development, not the other way around. Budgeting first and then developing goals and activities to fit is not unlike the work of an incompetent tailor.

To create a garment, a competent tailor carefully designs or selects a pattern for the type of garment requested, measuring carefully to determine the amount of fabric needed. The tailor then obtains the necessary amount of fabric and proceeds to make the garment according to the pattern. This is a logical and appropriate sequence of the process. The cloth is cut to fit the pattern.

However, school systems often have budgeted contrary to the method of the tailor. Sometimes, the amount of money is determined and allocated to system units and schools. The units and schools then have a known amount of resources (the "cloth") and proceed to create and build an effective school (the "garment"). Unfortunately, the needs of the school may exceed the financial allocation provided, so the school has to cut and eliminate programs and services (leave out part of the "garment"). The pattern (needs) has to be cut to fit the cloth. Admittedly, this makes little sense, but it is a very real example of how many school systems expect certain outcomes but do not couple the necessary resources to deliver the desired product.

To assure that the educational system is operating in a sensible manner in planning and budgeting, the following checklist of characteristics of quality of planning is provided for consideration (Downey, Steffy, Poston, & English, 2009).

Checklist of Quality in Planning Design and Delivery

- ❏ **Policy Expectations**. The governing body of the system has placed into policy the expectation that the superintendent and staff think collectively about the future and that this thinking should take some tangible form without prescribing a particular template, allowing for flexibility as needed.
- ❏ **Visionary/Direction.** Leadership has an implicit or explicit vision of the general direction for where the organization is going for improvement purposes, which emerges from consideration of the organizational future.

- ❑ **Data Driven.** Data influence the planning and system direction and initiatives.
- ❑ **Budget Sequence.** Budget planning for change is done in concert and as a part of other planning, with goals and actions from those plans driving the budget planning process.
- ❑ **Day-to-Day Decisions.** Leadership makes day-to-day decisions regarding the explicit or implicit direction of the system and facilitates movement toward the planned direction.
- ❑ **Emergent/Fluid Planning.** Leadership adjusts for discrepancies between current status and desired status, facilitates movement toward the desired status, and is fluid in planning efforts (emergent in nature).
- ❑ **Deliberate Articulated Actions.** Staff members are involved in a purposeful way through such efforts as school/unit improvement planning, professional development councils, and district task forces, which are congruent with the coherent and articulated direction of the system or system initiatives.
- ❑ **Professional Development Alignment.** Professional development endeavors are aligned to system planning goals and initiatives.

System planning needs to meet these standards in order to be a viable and useful tool for school systems. Each of the criteria in the checklist impacts the quality of a system's operational progress over time, and leaders need to be mindful of the constructive consequences that materialize when planning processes reflect the quality planning criteria.

SUMMARY OF BUDGET PLANNING

It is apparent that successful and effective organizations have something in common. Success requires careful preparation for an uncertain future; it also needs budgeting, unity of effort, operational activities, and resource allocations to be driven by the system's needs and purposes. Without a conceptualization of where the organization is compared to where it wants to be, the system loses strength in its resolve to be successful. Planning needs to be an ongoing, continuous process. It must constantly respond to emerging needs of the organization, the organization's successes and failures, and the changes requisite in the nature of the organization's work and be empirically coupled with available resources. Without skilled planning, the threat of creeping mediocrity is likely to become a reality within even the best-intentioned organization.

4

Budgeting for Financial Prudence and Productivity

There are workshops and conferences every year for educational leaders and policy makers on how to build a financially prudent, but productive, organization. However, the choices to be made are often clouded with misperceptions. For example, when school budget cuts focus on superficial things like supplies, the action may actually produce skepticism about whether the amount of money for supplies was needed in the first place. Most would be skeptical that teachers could do without pencils and paper or notebook computers and software. Whether money matters is more important than what it buys. The way out of this dilemma is for schools to specify which students receive what, using which resources, and in which programs. Think of productivity as "throughput." Money will make a difference only when the staff, training, activities, or other resources the system acquires matter—beyond what is being spent, but what results are being achieved.

Economic confidence for public institutions was defined in Chapter 1 as a juxta-position of financial prudence (using funds effectively), financial alignment (living within available means), and performance (tying results to funding and increasing productivity). All public institutions, including school systems, are in large measure dependent upon public support, not only of their intended purpose and mission but also for public funding supplied by taxes or other revenues. A school system's credibility in its operational success and its financial affairs is critical for the system's very survival in a democratic society. Achieving economic confidence for public institutions is a major challenge at best and a threat to continued existence at worst.

PUBLIC INSTITUTIONAL BUDGETING NEEDS

For decades, public institutional approaches to budgeting were well established with little change from year to year, and the process was highly predictable with budget increases over time made in a politically determined manner (Wildavsky & Caiden, 1997). This approach involved small steps, and the budget-building process was often anchored in historical funding levels and focused on small, steady increases and growth. Decision makers were inclined to follow the tendency of government to tinker with policies rather than to question the value of continuing them (Högye, 2002).

Many school administrators refer to the phenomenon of "budget creep" as programs and services—once established—continue to be funded again and again with small budget increases without any reexamination of the value or results from the activity. In recent years, attempts have been made to monitor program results in order to further program accountability. It goes without saying that public institutions are responsible to publicly identify, track, and measure the efficacy of how all public monies vested in them are utilized. However, budget processes generally miss this important step—the ongoing evaluation of program costs and benefits and reconsideration of the necessity of the program's results. Reform measures in legislative bodies have prompted school organizations to acknowledge that just because a program was established in years past is no longer a guarantee of its necessity or future existence.

Public school budgeting needs to be congruent with standard expectations found in public rules and norms, including the following selected and summarized classical principles (Howard, 1973, pp. 5–8, as cited in Mikesell, 1991, p. 121):

Inclusiveness. All revenues and expenditures connected to the activities of the system are included.

Unity. All expenditures (regardless of purpose) and all revenues (regardless of source) need to be clearly linked together and consistently evaluated accordingly.

Fidelity. Budget allocations, once incorporated into the adopted budget, must not be changed during a given budget year except for documented and endorsed critical considerations approved by the governing authority.

Accuracy and clarity. Budget assumptions and forecasts must be soundly based upon reasonable information, and budget descriptions must be easily understood by the constituents of the organization, including patrons of the system.

Transparency and openness. Budgets must include full, complete, and fastidiously accurate information about expected revenues and planned expenditures that is open to the public with utmost integrity.

Without the preceding principles or rules, it would be difficult to further accountability in educational institutions. The need for public disclosure and support demands attention in any public institution's budgeting process.

BUDGETING IMPLICATIONS FOR EDUCATIONAL ORGANIZATIONS

School organizations are unique public institutions and perhaps one of the closest, if not the closest, form of government to the people of a given community. Schools are often neighborhood centers for students, parents, patrons, and others; and the system often finds that it serves a wide variety of publics. In order to focus the organization in accordance with those diverse needs, budgeting provides a decision-making paradigm for operational functions. A few of the components of the paradigm include the following:

Organizational focus. School system budgeting responds to the diagnosed needs of its clientele and community. The budget may be constructed in various ways, but its focus is on the needs it identifies and the types of programs and services it must develop and deliver.

Perpetual change. Change may be gradual, but it continues persistently over time and informs the school system of how its budget needs to be constructed to modify its mission in order to serve emerging requirements of a changing clientele.

Organizational harmony. Once direction is determined, the budgeting process for school systems is a useful tool for structuring the implementation of objectives over a reasonable time horizon and with coordination and harmony across organizational units and operations.

Results-based. The budget must be used to measure results and costs, in order to provide comprehensive and useful data for decision making. An important dimension of this perspective is that the budgeting strategy must avoid a common defect by not focusing on what is being *purchased*. Rather, it is essential that the system focuses on what is being *achieved* (Chabotar, 1987).

Monitoring performance. Improving organizational performance over time requires monitoring of functions and operations with an eye toward satisfaction of needs of clientele and community. Management cannot choose to ignore this important responsibility in a dynamic organizational context found in school organizations.

Of course, implementation of the budget in school systems is not without its problems and issues. For example, any allocation system—regardless of type—provides an arena for organizational activities to compete for scarce resources. There are always more needs to be served than there is funding to serve them, so some things are included in the budget and some things are left out. The decision to set priorities for selecting the activities to be funded or not funded and at what level is highly difficult.

PRODUCTIVITY IMPROVEMENT STRATEGIES FOR SCHOOL SYSTEMS

The aim in productivity action is to improve the organization's results within available resources—often stagnant or diminishing. The strategies address the need to get more output out of the inputs of the system. Most strategies fall into four categories:

1. Revenue enhancement

2. Expenditure reduction

3. Operational efficiencies

4. Abandonment and prioritization

Taking these strategies in order, there are considerations that school systems have employed to effect some realization and success with each.

Revenue Enhancement

Several actions are available to school systems for enhancing or augmenting revenues. A sampling of this type of productivity improvement is found in the following list of suggestions:

1. Build a reasonable cash reserve for the system. This may sound out of place, but many school systems have minimal or no reserves. In such situations, the reserves are not sufficient for handling periodic financial obligations of the system. To pay its bills, the system may be obligated to borrow funds or register warrants resulting in additional expense and interest paid to a lending institution. This is something that can be avoided with an adequate cash reserve, with which systems may accrue revenue from earned interest on their unexpended funds at various times when balances permit.

2. Consider establishing an educational foundation. Tax deductions accrue to individuals and/or corporations that contribute funds to a qualified independent nonprofit foundation. Foundations may solicit contributions and conduct fundraising activities to build a body of funds that may be used for charitable purposes—in this case, used for schools. Some school communities have raised millions of dollars through educational foundations, which choose to provide monetary and program support to the system. Of course, governance of the foundation must comply with state and federal law, and the officers of the organization must be independent of the school system—responsible for determining how its resources are disbursed.

3. *Share facilities with other organizations.* School facilities are frequently vacant during evening hours, weekends, and summer months, making them excellent candidates for use by other organizations. Some schools have rented facilities to churches, clubs, athletic organizations, service groups, and hobby groups. Typically, the system revenues balance out the normal cost of operation of the facility, which includes utilities, maintenance and cleaning, depreciation, and other costs. Another option is for school systems to share facilities with other governmental agencies. This might include governmental programs like Meals on Wheels (meal preparation for indigent elderly), senior citizen center activities, and parks and recreation (i.e., split costs and share the use of swimming pools, playing fields, etc.).

4. *Operate programs with outside third parties.* Some programmatic involvement of schools is tangential from the central purpose of the school system, but sometimes the best institution to provide a service or program is the school system itself. For example, many communities have a need for before- and afterschool child care, which easily can be provided within school system facilities. Some systems have contracted with outside firms or organizations to manage the service or program on a fee-for-services basis, compensating the school system for use of its facilities and matériel. One system in Phoenix, Arizona, contracted with the local YMCA to provide afterschool child care for parents who were unable to be at home when their children returned from school; the program, including provision of a nutritious snack, was managed within school system buildings.

5. *Create a fee structure for optional program enrollment.* Some programs, related to the needs of students but not vital to the educational program of studies, may be provided on an elective basis for a fee. Examples found in school systems today include summer schools, driver's education, transportation services for noneligible students, recreational programs, and so on. The optional programs operate as quasi-independent entrepreneurial firms (on a profit–loss basis) and may provide additional revenues to the system.

6. *Seek and procure supplemental outside funding.* Many school systems aggressively seek and procure outside funding for programs and services. Grants and contracts, business partnerships, foundations, and other opportunities are sought vigorously in some instances. For example, several school systems in Mississippi obtained millions of dollars from a Japanese auto manufacturer locating in their area, with the funds aimed at improving the quality of schooling in that venue.

7. *Recruit tuition students.* In many states, enrollment in school systems is on an "open enrollment" basis. That is, students may choose to attend school systems other than their system of residence, if the recipient school system chooses to accept them and can meet their needs. In some states where this is common and

state aid follows the student to the new system, school systems are placed in the position of actually competing for student enrollments. Some school systems recruit and accept hundreds of nonresident students for state aid only. However, additional tuition costs may be assessed to nonresident students in some instances.

8. Plan and implement an aggressive investment program. This option, for cash reserves and unexpended, unallocated funds, requires careful consideration and circumspect discretion. Investment strategies in a dynamic economy always include some level of risk, but returns on investments may augment school system revenues if cautious considerations suggest that benefit outweighs the risk.

Most school systems have been limited to investing in legislatively prescribed investment vehicles including growth opportunities (domestic equities and international equities), income opportunities (bonds, private equity, and fixed income, such as U.S. Treasuries), real estate, and short-term cash. Not surprisingly, investments by public institutions are often governed by law; but an astute governing body may have the capability to adopt a policy to provide for diversification of assets in an effort to maximize investment returns to the system consistent with prudent levels of market and economic risk. Consideration of this alternative to enhance revenues demands thoroughly careful examination before a decision is made.

Expenditure Reduction

On the spending side of the financial management of school systems, a plethora of structural options or operational alternatives have been identified as available for consideration. Many of these have often been featured as special presentations at educational financial management conferences and conventions. Two categories are commonly noted in school systems—across-the-board reductions and targeted reductions. Both have advantages and disadvantages.

Across-the-Board Reductions—The Downside

Across-the-board reductions in budgets have advantages, but they also have serious disadvantages. Across-the-board cutting is defined as a uniform percentage or dollar reduction in all programs and activities within a school system. For example, the governor of Iowa mandated in the fall of 2009 that due to revenue shortfalls, all departments and agencies in state government would need to cut their planned budget for the current year by 10%. It was, as one pundit described it, "one size fits all."

Across-the-board cuts do have the advantage of timeliness—it takes little time to effectuate the cuts, and it is expedient in the short term. This type of expenditure reduction may be perceived as fair and uniform; but actually it is not equitable, just easier. In reality, across-the-board cuts diminish quality unevenly, and perpetuate—even protect—the status quo by eliminating the need for evaluation.

In the Iowa governor's plan, all departments were affected, but some more critically than others. One unintended consequence was that the Departments of Public Safety and Corrections were likely to lose hundreds of law enforcement officers, jeopardizing the safety and well-being of the citizenry. Another unintended consequence was that the Department of Justice, after losing large numbers of judicial personnel, was unable to handle the mushrooming criminal and civil caseloads of the state. Those effects were widely perceived as "penny wise" but "pound foolish." The across-the-board cutting approach also had a less-critical effect on some other departments. In effect, across-the-board cutting approaches unintentionally erode the capacity of critical functions to carry on and gradually reduce quality overall in essential *and* nonessential areas. In addition, restoration may or may not be likely in the future.

Generally, it is preferable to use "targeted" expenditure reductions, using evaluations of essentiality and performance to guide decisions to leave some things out of the budget. This helps develop efficiencies, explore paradigm shifts in service delivery, and improve the organizational structure. Targeted cuts are more difficult; but with focus on the main mission of the system, quality and essential activities can be better protected.

Types of targeted reductions, which are far less debilitating and allow abandonment of unessential or ineffective activities, are presented in the following section.

Targeted Reductions—A Positive Side

While by no means complete, selected examples of ways and means to reduce expenditures are presented for consideration.

Reduction of staffing. The most controversial suggestion is also the most substantial option available to school systems. Considering that sometimes as much as 90% of the school system's budget is comprised of personnel, this area of the budget is by default one of the most appealing options. School systems are service organizations, and they are highly labor intensive. Finding cost reductions in the area of personnel and staff is not trouble free, but there are things that can be considered.

Some school systems have used changes in pupil–teacher ratios to effectuate reduced cost. One school district in Montana found that increasing class size ratios by one student (from 21:1 to 22:1) saved close to one million dollars.

Other school systems have used early retirement incentives to encourage senior employees to retire early, enabling the system either to replace the employee with a lower-salaried and less-experienced employee or not to fill the resulting vacancy. Incentives have included bonus payments to escalate the amount of retirement income, extensions of subsidized health insurance for a set period, and other inducements.

Still other systems have chosen to "de-professionalize" some positions, thereby reducing cost. Examples include replacing professional, elementary librarians with classified employees with library training, who were called "library technicians"; replacing professional, study hall supervisors with classified paraprofessionals; replacing professional, teacher-coaches with part-time college graduates from the community with athletic qualifications; hiring noncertificated teachers in specialized areas such as industrial education and limited English proficiency courses.

Consolidation and economizing facilities and services. Generally, consolidation of programs and services seeks to reduce cost duplication between related programs. For example, in one Iowa university that had two separate colleges—one in consumer and family sciences and another in education—the two colleges had related, but completely separate, operations. By consolidating the two colleges, the need for duplicate administrative staffing, maintenance services, student support programs, and so on were eliminated. The operational cost savings obtained by consolidating the two schools was considerable.

Sharing. In public schools, occasionally two schools may be consolidated with a common principal and other support staff (librarian, maintenance, etc.), while the two schools remain on separate sites with separate student bodies. A school district in Arizona actually placed two separate elementary schools in one building, sharing facilities and support staff. One school's schedule ran from 7:00 a.m. to noon, and the other school's schedule ran from 12:30 p.m. to 5:30 p.m. The cost savings in facilities was in excess of several million dollars for a couple of years until the system could afford to build and staff a second school.

Construction. Construction of school facilities may have some little known opportunities for economizing simply in design. For example, a middle school in Arizona was constructed of 12-sided buildings (dodecagons) containing six classrooms. The area inside the buildings was about 7000 square feet, and the perimeter was about 300 feet. Surprisingly, if a square building were to be used with the *same* interior space, the perimeter would have been about 11.5% longer. Given the cost of constructing masonry walls is dictated by the cost per lineal foot, it actually was cheaper to construct the classroom buildings in the dodecagon shape. Using this cost savings in construction takes advantage of one of those anomalies in mathematics with polygons.

School closure. Obviously, an ultimate consolidation in schools is closure of one or more buildings and moving the student population to another school that has capacity to hold the enlarged enrollment. According to many systems' experience, that is generally easier said than done.

Deferral of maintenance and equipment replacement. Deferral of maintenance often has deleterious consequences for a school district. Eventually, maintenance problems must be dealt with, and the delay may contribute to a greater cost or a more complicated and difficult, as well as a more expensive, remedy. Nevertheless, when resources are extremely limited, some school systems have found that deferral of repairs, refurbishment, or replacement may help prevent elimination of more important programs or services.

While generally not advisable, use of this option occasionally may help offset other, less preferred, budget reductions; but any deferral of maintenance or equipment replacement must be clearly looked upon as only a temporary measure. Not paying for maintenance today will definitely require paying for maintenance tomorrow.

Energy cost controls. Costs for energy have mushroomed in recent years. In 2005, Americans spent $1 trillion on energy, over $200 billion more than the previous year. Prices will continue to rise, according to the Secretary of Energy. As evidence of this trend, between 2005 and 2006, the national growth rate for energy costs increased from 17% to 23%. School systems as users of these resources will face long-lasting problems as this crisis continues (U.S. House of Representatives, 2006).

Accordingly, the need for energy conservation has never been greater. One action taken by schools is to invoke centralized thermostat control of heating, ventilation, and air conditioning, which uses an automated system to manage thermostat settings with systemwide programming to minimize energy consumption.

Alternative forms of heating and cooling have also been implemented. Geothermal systems (which use constant temperature deep ground water for heating and cooling) and under-floor heating systems reduce the need for energy substantially. Many schools are utilizing these systems to genuinely diminish costs.

Other school systems have established electrical power self-generation with wind-powered electrical generation approaches. Of course, the capital investment at the front end of such a project is extraordinary, but the savings obtained are expected to amortize the investment in a small number of years.

Another approach involves constructing the school buildings in energy-saving ways. Using insulated concrete form (ICF) walls provides classroom walls that are highly energy efficient (R = 50). These "foam/concrete sandwich" walls are relatively inexpensive compared to the eventual energy cost savings obtained.

Moreover, constructing a school building partially underground also significantly reduces energy costs. Richardson Elementary School in Tucson, Arizona (Flowing Wells Public Schools) is such a building, and the insulation of the surrounding earth dramatically reduces heating and cooling costs.

One more method to reduce energy costs is by designing and implementing an unconventional schedule that doesn't require heating and cooling every day. For example, this plan suggests that if each school day were lengthened by 25% of the number of minutes in the normal instructional day, the schools would then be closed on the fifth day of each week, with a rollback of thermostat levels for the three-day weekend and a cost savings of realistic proportion. If the school day is normally 360 minutes, the day would be lengthened 90 minutes, making the school day seven and one half hours instead of six hours in length. Not having to heat the empty buildings at normal levels when the classrooms are not in use would reduce energy spending considerably.

Outsourcing. Many school systems have aggressively utilized outsourcing of operational functions in order to save money, and there have been mixed results. Outsourcing extends from very simple functions, such as equipment maintenance, to highly complex functions, such as operating schools with private management. As an example, the School District of Philadelphia outsourced the management of 28 of its schools to private firms in an attempt to improve the quality of achievement in underperforming schools. Privately managed schools make up nearly 10% of the 284 schools in that system.

The most common types of outsourcing are in the area of auxiliary services, usually tangential to the central mission of the system like food services, transportation, cleaning, and other support functions. These support services often are considered better operated by qualified outside private firms instead of by educationally trained school administrators. However, the experience for some school districts hasn't always been a positive one, as some school systems have tried outsourcing, only to eliminate it after a reasonable trial.

There are advantages to outsourcing. Aims and purposes for outsourcing programs and services generally focus on the following expectations: (1) less cost in operations, (2) transfer of risk, and (3) productivity enhancement.

1. Less cost in operations. Private management companies may operate more economically than an independent school system, due to economy of scale and superior expertise. One school system in Phoenix outsourced its food service program to the Marriott Corporation, which resulted in less cost due to the large volume of food service operations Marriott operated in hospitals, industrial firms, and a large university in the region. In this case, economy of scale reduced the operational cost of food services for the school system, and the school system's subsidy of the entrepreneurial food service program was eliminated due to efficiencies and quality of service.

One school system in Montana outsourced its transportation program to the Ryder Corporation, which not only had greater economy of scale but greatly increased expertise and skill in large fleet operations and computerized scheduling. Expense for operating transportation was reduced, especially when it came to bus replacement with much more favorable purchasing terms.

2. Transfer of risk. Any work performed in any organization carries with it the possibility of liability exposure and risk. In the event of outsourcing, private contracting firms generally provide for their own liability exposure and worker compensation with insurance coverage. For example, if tree-trimming is outsourced from a school system to a private firm, it is highly likely that the private firm would have greater expertise in trimming trees, better equipment, and less liability exposure. Even in a case of mishap, the private firm normally has assumed all risks.

3. Productivity enhancement. Outsourcing can provide a school system, especially a smaller system, with access to a larger pool of workers, specialized levels of expertise, and use of better technology. The opportunity to obtain more, accomplished with less time and effort, is greatly enhanced.

There is an abundance of measures that school systems have used or can use in reducing costs. The preceding list is perhaps only scratching the surface for school systems' options in expenditure reductions. However, the third area for consideration in this discussion is in the area of operational efficiencies.

Operational Efficiencies

Closely related to the expenditure reduction strategies, efficiencies invoke a broader view and more comprehensive implementation; and a paradigm shift may be called for in the manner of conducting the business of the school system.

Some examples of efficiencies include the following.

Privatization of whole operations. Akin to outsourcing, privatizing calls for a more significant movement of functions to private businesses. Included are such things as contracting with private firms to operate schools or contracting for payroll and benefits management, accounting and auditing services, subcontracted positions and responsibilities (such as teaching), and similar operations.

Participation in cooperatives. Many school systems have joined together to provide services to the enlarged group collaborative organization, including functions like joint purchasing and procurement for volume breaks in prices paid, self-insurance group organizations, shared transportation services, shared waste management and recycling operations, shared information technology services, and shared facilities and equipment. This allows the organization's member school systems to benefit from the larger group identity for some functions and services.

Wage and benefit constraints. Recent hard times in the economic marketplace have revealed some unusual creativity in addressing the pressure for retrenchment or staff layoffs. Some firms and governmental agencies have employed ostensibly temporary measures like reduced work weeks, employee short-duration furloughs without pay, deferral of some benefit obligations such as employer retirement contribution limits, increased levels of employee benefits cost-sharing, and automation for some functions (some schools use computers to call parents with information about their child's attendance in school), and others.

The abundance of cost savings measures is extensive. Any rational organization considering any of the suggested efficiency strategies needs to carefully connect a validly identified organizational need with a scrupulous evaluation of advantages and disadvantages before any strategy is deployed.

Abandonment and Prioritization

The poignant reality for public institutions is that resources always fall short of needs, requests, or demands. It is no secret that school systems are overburdened with underfunded demands and expectations to meet too many social needs (Rogers, 2007). The mushrooming costs for unfunded mandates also have a detrimental effect on local taxpayers. The escalation of legislative mandates without adequate funding has risen to such a magnitude that the New York Legislative Assembly was considering a bill at the time of this writing to identify unfunded mandates in proposed legislation because the mandates have resulted in the proliferation and rapid growth of property taxes (New York Assembly, 2009).

School systems in recent years have been inundated with a series of unprecedented state and federal initiatives and extraordinary demands for accountability, but funding for the spread of initiatives has been inadequate—with major revenue shortfalls and tight financial constraints in meeting the demands, requirements, and requests. The political environment presumably limits the capability of school systems to obtain additional funding to accomplish all the expectations, although the need for educational reform may be valid and justifiable.

However, that still leaves school systems with a dilemma—how to meet educational needs in the face of insufficient resources. It is obvious that in all likelihood it is an unattainable undertaking. Where then is the answer? Without adequate funding to meet all of its valid and identifiable needs, school systems have little choice other than to consider abandonment or restructuring of activities in order to get alignment between activities and resources available.

Abandonment

Abandonment is the process of choosing not to continue all or part of an activity for various reasons. Abandonment of an activity could be a possibility if financial means are not sufficient to support the activity. Another reason could also be the natural result of an evaluation that confirmed that the activity was unsuccessful or ineffective. For example, some years ago, a program that provided computers for young students to write was thought to help students learn to read. Evaluations of the program found it to be less than successful, so the program was abandoned or terminated in most systems.

Restructuring

Restructuring is the procedure to modify or adapt an activity in order to deliver the activity in a different manner, with the intent to maintain or improve results with less cost. For example, studies have confirmed that achievement improves, given changes in teachers' classroom organization. If teachers use cooperative grouping procedures, a positive effect on overall learning is achieved (Starcevich, 1990).

Cooperative learning calls for teachers to change their classroom design of student group work—organizing the group's work around the core components of cooperative learning. These components include positive interdependence, group processing, appropriate use of social skills, face-to-face interaction, and individual and group accountability. This modification of the work has noteworthy probability for augmenting learner achievement (Marzano, Pickering, & Pollock, 2001).

This change in learning activities is an example of the improvement of productivity—there was improved quality of product without additional cost.

Accordingly, restructuring efforts look for different and/or better ways to perform a function or conduct an activity that improves accomplishment of objectives within the constraints of existing resources.

Other restructuring examples may diminish outcomes or expectations to fit within available, albeit insufficient, resources. While this resembles "cutting the pattern to fit the cloth" (see Chapter 1), sometimes it is the most viable choice for a school system when there is no option for additional funding.

Examples might include restructuring the library services program from a professionally staffed library program five days a week to two or three days a week. The program might provide a paraprofessional or community volunteers on the days the library isn't staffed with a professional librarian. The activity modification is less desirable, but it does provide a degree of service and it costs less to implement. Another example might be to reduce daily cleaning services to three or four times a week instead. This also is less desirable, but it reduces cost and continues some level of service.

System Productivity

Whatever approach a system takes in forming and adopting a budget, it is important that the spotlight is on improving system quality and productivity. The system needs to focus on the following elements to make progress in enhancing organizational productivity.

- Financial parameters need to remain constant in planning to avoid dependence upon revenue growth and to eliminate spending driven by resource availability.
- Interventions, innovations, or changes in organizational operations and functions need to demonstrate that performance improved (or will improve) over time or face restructuring and/or termination.
- Budget proposals must document evidence of planned and actual congruence between system objectives and budget allocations, with specific means identified to attain improved results over time.
- Sound and relevant assessment feedback needs to drive participatory decision making with key instructional personnel involved.
- Objective and independent data need to prevail over politicization in decision making, and decisions and allocation changes need to be based on measured results or performance.

SUMMARY

The journey to prudence and efficiency takes many divergent paths, each laden with obstacles and benefits in varying degree. This chapter delineates many options for cost reductions and revenue enhancements, but careful consideration of all alternatives is suggested for greater assurance of success in maintaining or advancing quality in delivering success in learning to every learner.

5

Organizing and Goal Setting for Performance-Based Budgeting

Failing to connect plans with budgeting can have disastrous results. Consider the Nogales (Arizona) School District that built a new multimillion dollar high school some years ago. The new building had to sit vacant for over a year because the school board had neglected to budget for furnishings and equipment. Leadership planning in that situation was an embarrassment, to say the least.

Performance-based school system budgeting is set apart by its distinctive elements from school system budgeting in general. In this discourse, four types or categories of budgeting are recognized and explained to assure understanding of what performance-based budgeting looks like, how its elements are unique, and what it may accomplish. It's important to note that all four types share some common elements, but each type has distinctive characteristics setting it apart from the others.

FOUR TYPES OF BUDGETING APPROACHES

The differences in the major types of school system budgeting approaches include line-item or function-object budgeting, activity or program budgeting, incremental program budgeting, and performance-based budgeting.

Line-Item or Function-Object Budgeting.

In this traditional approach, which is the most widely used approach to school system budgeting, anticipated costs and items are organized by the function (i.e., instruction, support services, facilities acquisition, etc.). In effect, line-item budgeting describes the planned financial system in terms of what the money will purchase, such as salaries, supplies, utilities, equipment, and so on.

Typically, line-item budgets are developed from prior budget expenditures and revenues, but frequently without reconsideration of previously funded programs and services in terms of their efficacy and necessity to the system's mission.

Some advantages of using line-item budgeting are found in the system's considerable flexibility in the amount of control over various uses. Budget increases are often determined by simple formulas, such as a set amount per student for each school or a predetermined level of percentage as an increase. This approach usually budgets by school or departmental units, which enables monitoring expenditure information at each school, department, or level in the system. Most states and provinces require submitted budgets to accommodate the line-item approach.

There are also disadvantages with line-item budgeting approaches. Because it is a financial model which presents proposed funding by category or line item, it is difficult to identify the justifications for expenditures, and the information does not aggregate expenditures by goal, objective, or program information. It speaks to what the money "buys" in an obtuse way rather than what the money produces in terms of cost-benefit relationships, intended organizational purposes, or end results.

An example of a line-item budget is illustrated in Exhibit 5.1.

In line-item budgeting, the types of expenditures are categorized and tabulated often by units, such as schools or departments. Unfortunately, it's difficult to connect the expenditure objects with the organizational activity within which the line items reside, but the line items can be included in the next level of budgeting under consideration—program or activity budgeting, which does organize costs by the purpose or goals of the system.

Program or Activity Budgeting.

In this more descriptive approach, the budgeting process organizes costs by the specific program or activity with clear relationships between costs, actions taken or to be taken, and the planned aims and purposes of the activity. Programs or activities are linked to strategic goals, after which the costs of the activities needed are used to create the budget.

Activity-based budgeting stands in contrast to traditional, line-item budgeting practices, in which a prior year's budget is simply adjusted to account for inflation or revenue growth. Program or activity budgeting fosters a capability to align activities with objectives, make the activity more efficient, and improve business practices. This is a different focus, which simply describes expenditures for an activity with the means to measure and evaluate outcomes. Program budgeting is an improvement over the line-item approach because it is organized around what the money "does" and what the costs are for achieving the activity's goals. The program or activity budget bases expenditures on anticipated outcomes as

Exhibit 5.1   Line-Item Budget Planning Worksheet

Function: Instruction			
Object	Prior Year Budget	Prior Year Actual Expenditure	Next Year Proposed Budget
100 Salaries			
110 Regular Salaries			
120 Temporary Salaries			
130 Overtime Salaries			
140 Compensated Absence Salaries			
150 Early Retirement Incentives			
190 Other Salaries			
Total Salaries			
200 Employee Benefits			
Health Insurance			
FICA			
Other			
Total Employee Benefits			
300 Purchased Services			
310 Professional and Technical Services			
320 Property Services			
330 Transportation Services			
340 Communication			
350 Advertising			
360 Printing and Binding			
370 Tuition Paid			
390 Other Purchased Services			
Total Purchased Services			
400 Supplies and Materials			
410 Supplies			

(Continued)

Exhibit 5.1 (Continued)

Function: Instruction			
Object	Prior Year Budget	Prior Year Actual Expenditure	Next Year Proposed Budget
420 Textbooks			
430 Library Media			
440 Periodicals			
490 Other Supplies and Materials			
Total Supplies and Materials			
500 Capital Acquisitions			
510 Land			
520 Buildings			
530 Improvements Other Than Buildings			
540 Equipment			
550 Vehicles (licensed)			
560 Library Books			
590 Other Capital Expenditures			
Total Capital Acquisitions			
600 Other Objects			
610 Redemption of Debt Principal			
620 Interest Paid			
640 Dues and Fees			
650 Insurance and Judgments			
660 Registration Fees			
670 Student Loan Matching Funds			
680 Student Scholarships			
690 Miscellaneous Objects			
Total Other Objects			
Totals			

opposed to functions and objects. All expenditures planned are related to the fundamental objectives of the defined activity.

A key feature of this approach is that the "horse is in front of the cart," with the horse being the guiding principle and the cart being the system response. The organization's goals and objectives are translated into a set of activities within a program unit, and those expectations and activities are used to establish the budget. This phenomenon, described earlier, appropriately utilizes the pattern (curriculum activity) to determine the amount of fabric (funding), instead of the other way around (English, 1987).

An obvious advantage is that with this approach, school systems are likely to attain their goals and objectives and track expenditures against accomplishments. However, possible disadvantages may impede success if the system isn't clear about its primary goals and objectives or if available cost data is not assigned to specific activities or programs. Regardless of a few limitations, program budgeting continues to grow in popularity because of its connectivity to the intents and purposes of school system activities.

The concept itself is uncomplicated and easy to understand. A school system first decides what curriculum programs and services it will provide. Once this is accomplished, the system defines three factors germane to the program: the goal, the objectives, and the strategies or performance measures to be used to determine whether the objective or goal is met. The major benefit of this process is that it provides a clear focus on what the system intends to do and emphasizes planned program performance and ultimate outcomes, as opposed to inputs and processes. The process of program budgeting enables school system patrons and parents to understand in simple functional terms what the school system is doing, what it's spending to do it, and how results will be measured—enabling cost-benefit analysis (National Association of State Budget Officers, 1997).

Program budgets also contain the underlying function-object code structures commonly used in school systems, but the costs are structured within individually defined and budgeted program activities systemwide. Examples of a few program area budget worksheets found in activity budgets are displayed in Exhibit 5.2.

Exhibit 5.2 Program/Activity Budget Planning Worksheet With Objects for 20xx–xx Budget

Program Activity	Prior Year Budget	Prior Year Actual Expenditure	Next Year Proposed Budget	Proposed FTE (Full-Time Equivalents)
0800 Prekindergarten				
303 Teacher Salaries*				
303 Teacher Assistant Salaries*				
303 Paraprofessional Assistant Salaries*				

(Continued)

Exhibit 5.2 (Continued)

Program Activity	Prior Year Budget	Prior Year Actual Expenditure	Next Year Proposed Budget	Proposed FTE (Full-Time Equivalents)
601 Materials and Supplies				
0800 Total				
0900 Kindergarten				
303 Teacher Salaries*				
303 Teacher Salaries*				
303 Teacher Assistant Salaries*				
601 Equipment				
601 Materials and Supplies				
303 Special Education Kindergarten Teacher Salaries*				
303 Special Education Kindergarten Teacher Assistant Salaries*				
0900 Total				
1300 English Language Learners				
303 Teacher Salaries*				
303 Teacher Assistant Salaries*				
701 Teaching Supplies (Elem)				
801 Teaching Supplies (HS)				
801 Consumable Workbooks				
401 Teaching Textbooks				
1300 Totals				
6900 Intramural Activities				
309 Intramural Stipends				
309 Intramural Hourly				
401 Materials and Supplies				
901 Intramural Equipment				
6900 Total				

Note: Salaries include benefits – See note on following page.

Exhibit 5.2 shows a budget expenditure planning instrument for only four program activities as an example of how program budgeting works. Each program activity also has underlying goals and objectives, and it generally contains all the incumbent costs systemwide for the program. See note below for information about costing positions.[1] School systems typically have 25 or more program activity areas included in their budget. With this format, it is also easier for the general public to grasp and ascertain where the school system's money actually goes, making a tangible connection between what the money buys and what it produces.

At another level, incrementally based budgeting was developed because of the uncertainties that school systems often face with fluctuating or stagnant revenues, unanticipated changes in community conditions, and rising expectations. In the event of diminishing revenues or unexpected emerging needs, school systems often have to reduce funding within their existing allocation structures in order to accommodate the unforeseen and nascent demands.

Incremental Program Budgeting

This approach to budgeting is actually a modification of zero-based budgeting, developed nearly five decades ago in private sector companies (including Ford Motor Company), championed in the Department of Defense under Robert McNamara in the early 1960s, and refined later for use by school systems (Bliss, 1978). Zero-based budgeting is a method of budgeting in which all expenditures are justified each new budget term, as opposed to simply requesting and describing amounts in excess of the previous term's budget. Basically, zero-based budgeting starts from a "zero base," and every program or operation within an organization is analyzed for its needs and costs. Budgets are then built around what is needed for the upcoming period, regardless of whether the budget is higher or lower than the previous one.

While zero-based budgeting can lower costs by avoiding blanket increases or decreases to a prior period's budget, it is not useful in school systems without adaptation. Schools perennially provide and conduct educational programs and services, and with few exceptions, said programs and services are not effortlessly rolled back to zero. Schools must continue, and resource support is assuredly likely to continue. Consequently, a modified approach requires that programs and services have alternative levels of funding with a redesigned program in accordance with funding available.

For example, if a school system is faced with reduced funding or anticipates less funding in future, the system plans ahead with contingency alternatives for each program that respond to different levels of funding. The levels might be of three general types:

---

[1] For ease in the program level or budgeting process, positions—such as teachers, custodians, bus drivers, and so on—may be budgeted as discrete components. Salary, benefits, travel, allowances, and the like are totaled and included in a single figure and averaged by type of position. Hypothetically, if there are only two teachers in the system, one costing $40,000 total and the other costing $60,000 total, the average for the imaginary system of two would be $50,000 per teaching position. That average would be used for each position (or all positions in actuality). Once programs are established, or unit (like schools) staffing is determined, the actual position allocations may be reconciled at the program or unit level for specific persons and position costs. This approach eliminates complicated accounting maneuvers during budgeting, but it provides for full inclusion of personnel position costs.

1. *Recovery*. Less funding than the previous year is anticipated and the educational program is redesigned accordingly. For example, the instrumental music program may commence at fourth grade in the current budget period; but if funding is anticipated to diminish, an alternative program is designed to fit within the reduced funding level that commences instrumental music at the sixth grade level, thereby "recovering" a portion of the previous budget terms' allocations for music for use elsewhere in the system or for abandonment. Recovery alternatives have ranged from 75% to 99% of the previous term's financing in school systems that have used the recovery level.

2. *Current or existing*. Funding is anticipated to remain constant from the previous budget term to the next, so funding levels for programs would remain at the current level. If there is an inflationary factor, the current level of funding may need increasing to incorporate the change in cost for the same program alternative or existing funding support in constant dollars.

3. *Enhancement.* Programs and services need to respond to enrollment growth, innovation, deficiencies in achievement, and a plethora of other factors. Realistically, in recent history, the major source of funding for improvement often has been found in the school system's previous allocations, which calls for use of recovery alternatives in some programs to acquire funds for reallocation to other programs. Enhancement alternatives are alternative program proposals that require greater funding because of a changing need. One school system in suburban Omaha funded a 322% enhancement alternative in its computer education program in order to help get its technology programs up to the quality demanded in that rapidly changing field of endeavor. Of course, once that program alternative was funded and the equipment was obtained, the funds returned to the system for reallocation again.

The fundamental result of incremental budgeting is the reconsideration and possible elimination of outdated efforts and expenditures and the concentration of resources where they are most effective. This is achieved through an annual review of all program activities and expenditures, which results in improved information for allocation decisions. However, the process does demand more staff time, planning, and preparation.

Incremental budgeting, like all budgeting, involves competition for funding among programs and services. In determining whether or not a program is funded at the recovery, current, or enhanced level is a matter of priority setting. The process of determining priorities is discussed later in Chapter 7.

An example of an individual program's plan within an incremental budgeting approach is provided in Exhibit 5.3.

In incremental budgeting, all programs are identified, and each prepares a set of prescribed program components in accordance with the funding levels selected. The programs are then presented as three or more levels of quality for delivery of the program's services with clear distinctions between them. The quality determinations are used in developing the final budget proposal by rank-ordering

Exhibit 5.3   Incremental Budget-Planning Proposal for Music Program 20xx–xx Budget

	Budget Level		
	Recovery (90%)	Current (100%)	Enhancement (117%)
Program Components:	*Instrumental music starts in Grade 6*	*Instrumental music starts in Grade 4*	*String instruction starts in Grade 7 (new)*
Line Items:			
1900 Music (K–12)	Base Cost	Restore 10% of Previous Year	Add-On 17%
303 Teacher Salaries	$148460	$22,287	$37,115
301 Music Equipment	$73,400	$2,344	$7,895
801 Teaching Equipment	$3,482	$1,738	$700
301 Music Furniture	$5,088	$654	$1,955
401 Music Repairs	$1,400	$200	$400
801 Field Trip Expenses	$6,900	$0	$1,100
401 Materials and Supplies	$4,500	$612	$3,455
901 Consumable Workbooks	$5,500	$891	$1,750
801 Music Textbooks	$14,880	$564	$0
1900 Program Totals	**$263,610**	**$29,290**	**$54,370**

the various components across programs. A list of program component proposals is then created in order of priority. Once the amount of revenue is known, the rank-ordered components are approved for funding in order of priority to the extent that available funds permit.

This approach extends the tangible connection between a program's goals and its quality with the amount of funding, making it much easier to grasp how the organization's funds are allocated and for what purpose. In effect, patrons can see what the money does as well as how much money it is. This is definitely an open, transparent approach to budgeting since immersion in a blizzard of line items is avoided in lieu of a clear and coherent incremental programmatic approach where there are no surprises or mysteries in data analysis.

In many school systems, this tangible connection between funding needs and program quality has been used to help foster support for budget increases, program improvements, and tax overrides. In some cases, the configuration of the incremental budget has been instrumental in successful referenda when that option is available for obtaining funding from the system's constituency. The obvious advantage is that by offering different levels of program quality at different levels of funding, this type of budget assures a balance between the current revenues and current programs and services expenditures.

Other advantages include the opportunity for development of creative and alternate means for delivery of programs and services (i.e., internal transportation services vs. outsourced transportation services; normal heating, ventilation, and air conditioning systems vs. electronically monitored and managed use of utilities; professional library services vs. partial paraprofessional library services). Given the opportunity, the synergy of collaborative planning and development often not only enhances the quality of the program or service but also reduces the cost, which improves organizational productivity.

Performance-Based Budgeting

This type of budgeting approach adds a key operation for the educational organization—accountability. The performance-based budget is a tool that makes it possible to evaluate

- administrative management and organizational performance,
- efficiency and financial prudence in system operations, and
- effectiveness of system activities and functions in achieving organizational goals and objectives.

Performance-based budgeting calls for *a priori* determinations about what a given budgetary component, program, or service will accomplish and a definition of how the part will be measured and evaluated. In successive budgeting periods, the feedback on results is critical information in planning whether or not to continue, change, or conclude the program components. In effect, once the budget component is funded, it is held to its established goals and objectives, aims and purposes, and commitments to fiscal efficiency in implementation. The type of feedback information needs to be valid, robust, and convincing for budget planning and decisions. Unfortunately, many school system curriculum-management audits reveal that this ingredient is often missing or mismanaged.

Even after adopting and implementing educational programs, too seldom does the organization determine if the program is successfully accomplishing what it was created to do (Downey, Steffy, Poston, & English, 2009). For best use of limited resources, the evaluation piece is of profound importance for the improvement of productivity.

Structurally, the performance-based budget includes the features of the incremental budget with components built at differential levels of quality, but the major difference is the addition of addressing a question about consequences for each program component. For example, if the proposed component isn't funded, the question in budgeting is "so what?" What difference does it make?

Conversely, what is gained if the component is funded, and how will the organization document or determine its value?

Once the resultant outcome is designed and incorporated into the program budget proposal, subsequent budget period proposals would be able to examine the previous period's experience with the funded component in terms of its success. This information in turn helps the budget planning team to make decisions about the efficacy of the component and to consider possibilities for funding the program piece.

Specific instructions about planning and carrying out evaluation of program components are provided in Chapter 6.

Comparisons and Differences Among Types of Budgeting

In the following exhibit, the four types of budgets are compared against nationally published objectives for budgeting (National Center for Educational Statistics, 2004, chap. 3).

In Exhibit 5.4, the activity or program budget has advantages over the line-item budget, the incremental budget has advantages over activity or program budgeting, and performance-based budgeting has advantages over the incremental program budget approach. The differences range from descriptions of what funding may purchase, definitions of the purposes that the funding will serve, differences in quality related to funding, and rationally ascertaining the value of funding for a given program, service, or component therein.

Exhibit 5.4   Comparing Budget Types to Budget Objectives

Budget Objectives	Line-Item	Activity	Incremental	Performance
Compliance with federal, state, and local laws and requirements	x	x	x	x
Identification of sufficient of revenues for expenditures	x	x	x	x
Verification of use of resources within legally adopted budget	x	x	x	x
Facilitation of measurement of total program costs		x	x	x
Provision of choices among multiples levels of program quality			x	x
Implementation of evaluation of program results				x

PREPARING FOR ORGANIZATIONAL BUDGETING NEEDS

Rational organizations have defined purposes, prescribed work tasks, and assessment of progress toward established purposes. Rational organizations also structure policies to assure the following:

1. Documentation of organizational aims, purposes, expectations, and processes in writing to mitigate misunderstandings, confusion, or even litigation in organizational operations and performance

2. Continuity and consistency throughout the organization by delineating duties and responsibilities of the organization and consequences of various courses of action and by resolution of differences arising from individual discretion in decisions and actions

3. Institutionalization of practices and expectations with written and documented declarations of appropriate organizational and prescribed individual activities

Budgeting policy is also required for smooth and proper operation of the school system's financial management system. Without policy, functions and actions have little or no guidelines or direction within an organization and dissonance is highly likely to develop within the organization.

Designing and Adopting Policy for Budgeting

Two model policies for budgeting are available for use in performance-based budgeting situations. One is comprehensive and specific, and the other is concise and discretionary. The comprehensive and specific model policy is displayed in Exhibit 5.5.

As can be seen in the exhibit (5.5), this model policy clearly and comprehensively delineates the expectations of the governing board for the budgeting process—in this case, performance based. In the system adopting this policy, the board had carefully provided unambiguous guidelines for this system's budgeting process.

In another model policy shown in Exhibit 5.6, the system decided it best to provide the chief executive officer maximum discretion in preparing and managing the budget planning process. This second model policy, concise and discretionary, contrasts considerably with the first model policy.

How much discretion is appropriate for system policies? Every system is different, but there is a method to poll the school system's constituency to see what the collective judgment of the system might be. A diagnostic instrument to help the school system is located in Appendix B at the back of the book, and a set of guidelines for governing boards to consider is provided in Appendix A, if a board is interested in addressing the diagnosed needs. The results of the survey process

Exhibit 5.5   Model Policy I Financial Management: Budgeting

The governing board shall adopt a budget for the ensuing fiscal year in accordance with the requirements and schedule established by state statute. The board authorizes the superintendent to prepare a budget plan for recommendation to the board in a timely manner and in accord with legal requirements appertaining thereto. The superintendent shall plan and implement procedures necessary to prepare a budget for recommendation that includes the following characteristics:

- Definition and descriptions of services, programs, or operations in a format that clearly communicates the nature of the purpose and activity to be funded ("program/activity-based")
- A range of defined components or levels of quality or performance within a given service, program, or operations area and with at least three different levels of quality and corresponding cost ("incremental levels")
- Inclusion of measurement tools and criteria for evaluating the efficacy or value of the results expected from each incremental level of a given program ("assessment methodologies")
- Organization of the program components in rank order or priority based on the comparative worth of each component compared to the other components as determined by a budget planning body organized and supervised by the superintendent that includes principals, teachers, and others as determined by the superintendent ("stakeholder involvement")
- Detailed and complete cost information, including cost-benefit analyses, where feasible, about each service, program or operational area's component and anticipated outcome if funded ("total cost and value")

At the superintendent's discretion, the budget may also be prepared in a format which permits allocations and implementation of the budget in accordance with a school-based budgeting philosophy and plan in accordance with district standards and policies.

The superintendent shall prepare and present the recommended budget in summary list form, with all program, service, or operation components in priority order for consideration by the board. Each budget component shall include sufficient information to permit clear understanding and analysis of each component's purpose, characteristics including staffing and all other included items, expected results or consequences if funded or not funded, any information about functioning or cost/benefit relationships, and the total cost of a given component if funded.

The board shall take the recommendation of the superintendent under advisement and shall organize and rank order the budget components in accordance with the board's collective judgment of each service, program, or operation area component's worth to the district and its relationship to the mission and goals of the school system.

generally clarify the system's stakeholders' preferences about guidelines and structure of the budgeting process.

Objectives for Efficacy in Performance-Based Budgeting

The performance-based budgeting process is a departure from traditional budgeting approaches, but it addresses specific intentions and purposes based

Exhibit 5.6　Model Policy II Financial Management: Budgeting

The superintendent of schools is directed to formulate and recommend the performance-based annual budget to the board. A "performance-based" budget can be defined as a budget process whereby fund requests are organized by a given service, program, or operation area and are prioritized by goals and objectives, incremental levels of funding, and by program productivity results and cost efficiency. Priorities are set by participation of key stakeholders in accordance with the district decision-making process defined by the superintendent in accordance with district policy.

The superintendent shall ensure that resources are utilized and allocated to produce the best possible effect on the district mission, goals, and pupils within the resources available and the conditions under which the district must operate.

The superintendent shall be responsible for reviewing budget requests, providing guidelines and limitations, and presenting the proposed budget and documentation necessary for board study, review, and action in a timely manner.

Budget planning shall include consideration of all conditions imposed by state statute.

on an empirically based rationale. The process addresses the following six fundamental objectives:

1. Manage organizational change and socioeconomic needs.

   o School organizations, as pointed out earlier, continually have to deal with emerging initiatives, changing clientele, and vigorous uncertainty in social and economic climates.
   o Over time, organizational actions and activities need modification or adaptation to fluctuating community conditions.

2. Improve productivity with a resource recovery system for reallocation.

   o Many school budgeting processes accept previous allocations as a starting point for future funding decisions.
   o New, unanticipated programs, services, demographics, and innovations require resources in order to be successfully addressed.
   o Availability of growth in financial support is limited, which requires greater productivity in current uses of resources.
   o In some cases, the only funds a school system may have to meet an emerging and important need may be found only in currently available funds.

3. Maximize effectiveness of decision making with up-to-date assessment and group development.

   o Organizational effectiveness is substantially dependent upon accurate and valid information, which undergirds data-based decision making.
   o Participatory decision making has the advantage of eliciting more extensive information; therefore, more possible solutions to the situation may be generated.

- o Shared decision making builds shared responsibility for decisions and their results.
- o Involved people want clear and sufficient information from which to draw conclusions. Noninvolved people do not want to put effort into decisions.
- o Performance-based budgeting benefits from greater participation of parents, patrons, and employees in the decision-making processes (Petty & Cacioppo, 1986).

4. Demonstrate fiscal prudence in the use of public funds.

- o Efficiencies are very important in constructing school system budgets, and the structure of performance-based evaluation provides an advantage to improve cost-benefit relationships in organizational operations and fiscal management.
- o Evaluation of funded component efficacy, effectiveness, and efficiency is facilitated within performance-based budgeting, which in turn facilitates greater economy and effectiveness within the system.
- o Not all wants and needs can be satisfied as there are always more requests for funds than available funds can satisfy, requiring the use of priorities.

5. Build equity into resource reallocations and in the delivery of programs and services for equal success in learning for all students.

- o Some schools face a more challenging clientele and situation than other schools to ensure successful learning outcomes across the system (Ross & Levačić, 1999).
- o Needs are not uniform across schools, and allocations must be based on differential needs rather than on equal allocations to obtain equity—one size doesn't fit all.
- o Pupil achievement is strongly influenced by socioeconomic factors, including poverty rates, family fragmentation, and student job activities (Schick, DeMasi, & Green, 1992).
- o Socioeconomic factors can be overcome, given creative and differentiated curriculum and instructional responses tailored to the different needs of schools with differentiated resource funding (English & Steffy, 2001).

6. Focus organizational resources on programs and services crucial to pupil achievement.

- o School systems are complex organizations, but all system activities need to focus on the optimization of pupil learning for the entire system clientele.
- o Require all funding requests to specify operationally the nature of the objectives to be served and to clearly identify practicable methods and means for assessment.

o Connect all funding requests to the main mission of the system and build in measures to determine relevancy, quality, and cost-effectiveness prior to resource allocation.

o Collaboratively allocate priorities to funding requests in accordance with connectivity to the system mission, probability of success, and expected, measurable results.

o Follow up on previous allocations and monitor results in considering continued or modified funding.

Commencing a process for performance-based budgeting requires advance consideration by the decision-making body of what the objectives of the system are and how the system may attain those objectives. It's important to acknowledge that objectives are conceptualized and defined purposes, which may require broad, long-range commitment to be attained. It's also important to remember that some organizational responses to needs may be relatively expensive to initiate, but may be highly cost-effective after development over time.

For example, in Australia and New Zealand, the Reading Recovery program was expensive to implement initially; but such programs were found to reverse some of the social costs of failure, such as diminished tax revenues, increased unemployment costs, and criminal activity expense (Dyer, 1992).

It is not difficult for a complicated service delivery organization to become fragmented and dislodged from its original key central purpose. When organizational activities undermine the main mission of the school system, suboptimization occurs. In a sense, it's critical for school system decision makers to keep their "eye on the ball," meaning that thorough and careful scrutiny of funding requests is needed and all requests are to be judged on three factors before funding:

1. The relevance and criticality toward the organizational mission

2. The structure and nature of the request's activities and the suitability for reaching the system's goals

3. The availability of straightforward and authenticated data, which demonstrates results useful in evaluating each request before and after funding

Given financial constraints, not all requests can be funded; but those that are funded may be better constructed and developed to enhance the improvement of organizational effectiveness and productivity over time.

6

Constructing the Process for Performance-Based Budgeting

Participatory decision making isn't always popular. After sitting through a presentation on performance-based budgeting, one Minnesota superintendent said to the presenter, "I like this process, but can I do it without the team involvement?" Participatory decision making is often more complicated and difficult to make work, but experience shows that those who participate in performance-based budgeting favor principals' and teachers' participation by a huge margin.

Any organizational process, to be successful, needs to clearly plan many things in advance. Some of these system-planning needs include anticipation of what needs are to be met, who will be served, how the system's response will be structured, what activities will be required, when implementation will occur, and how it will be determined if the process was successful.

A budget is in reality developed from an organizational plan or set of goals. It is a financial strategy setting forth how revenues will be determined, where revenues will come from, how much may be allocated, which programs and services will use the funds, and how success will be measured. Moreover, the plan also includes a determination of how the system will make its choices and decisions regarding fund allocations.

ESTABLISHING THE BUDGET DEVELOPMENT SCHEDULE

Developing a performance-based budget involves a large number of actions and activities over an extended period of time. Experience has shown that a minimum of one year of advance planning and preparation is required; some school systems have mastered the process in less than a year, but not without difficulty.

The processes, activities, and actions to be taken will be delineated in this chapter and will include a suggested timeline for consideration.

Accumulating an Expenditure History and Experience (Starting Point—SP)

This first activity involves obtaining expenditure data and conducting an analysis of the previous year's data in order to build baseline cost information for each program to be developed and budgeted for the projected year. The senior financial operations officer is generally charged with responsibility for this task and given a month or so to complete the enumeration and tabulations.

The data need to be actual amounts spent in the previous budget period for each program center (see the next step) rather than budgeted amounts. If budgeted amounts for each program are used, the accuracy level diminishes because programs often expend less or more than the budgeted amounts. Budgets are not as useful in determining the actual level of financial support that a program might need. Budgets also are often estimates; but even with good information, the costs may not be accurately represented by the budgeted amount.

So all object codes relevant to a program need to be accumulated, identified, prorated across programs as needed, and enumerated as correctly as possible. Most financial reporting systems and software make this task less onerous than in the past, but some systems have found that simply aggregating costs by the program activity took in excess of a couple of months. More recent experience with automation and data-based systems has reduced the time commitment considerably.

The final product of this process would include the following parts:

- The program activity definition. What the program does, how it works, and what services or commodities were obtained as the result of a specific expenditure within a specific program.
- A comprehensive delineation of expenditures including personnel services, benefits, purchased services, technical services, purchased property services, supplies and materials, capital outlay (including equipment), debt-related costs, and other expenses related to the particular program.
- A list of all expenses categorized by object code. For more information on object codification, see Chapter 6 in the U.S. Department of Education publication on financial accounting for school systems (National Center for Educational Statistics, 2003).

Once these elements are determined, the resultant total would be the current or existing baseline cost for a given program in the previous budget period or year. With this information, the organizational leadership may proceed with identifying the specific programs that will be included in the budget preparation process for the ensuing year.

One additional task for the system is to create a codification system for use in identifying each program in such a manner that it can be used in the system's accounting structure. Some systems have used a two-digit or three-digit designator code unique to each program, which allows the program's financial allocations to be tracked or monitored within the system's database and during the budgeting process. The codification is strictly for local use in assigning funding to programs. A second designator is also created to apply to the increments or subcomponents of a program for ease of monitoring. That is more fully explained in step 5 of this process, which is explained later in this chapter.

Determining Program Areas and Appointing Program Managers (SP + one month)

After the expenditure amounts have been determined, it is then possible to move on to identifying which program areas will be combined and which will remain independent and stand alone. For example, some systems make kindergarten a separate program in this process, but other systems include kindergarten under an elementary instruction program. Either choice is acceptable, but of course, monitoring or tracking cost-benefit relationships for individual programs may require greater separation of programs. If that is not a concern with a given program, consolidation of programs is not a problem.

Usually, the more separate and unique programs the system designates, the more the system may be able to make evaluative judgments of program results and cost connections. Most school systems employing the process have no fewer than fifteen or twenty program areas initially, but systems may wish to designate fifty programs or more. Two lists of programs from two separate Minnesota school systems, one large and one small in size, are found in Exhibit 6.1. Note the numbers of programs, program nomenclature, and the distinctive nature of each of the designated program lists.

The larger system has designated twenty-one programs, and the smaller system identified sixteen program areas. District 2 has English as a second language as a program, but the other does not. District 2 separated out human resources and community education, but District 1 did not. Neither system separated out kindergarten, building administration (principals and office expense), or custodial services from maintenance services. How many separate program areas are desired is entirely within the discretion of the system.

Deciding Which Programs Need To Be Included

In the District 1 and 2 examples, the programs listed are selected by the administration from among those programs found wholly or partially within the general

Exhibit 6.1   Designated Program Areas for Two School Systems

Example District 1 (Enrollment 17,000)	Example District 2 (Enrollment 60,000)
Governance and Management	Elementary Instruction (K–6)
Business Services	Junior High Instruction (7–9)
District Support Services	Senior High Instruction (10–12)
Elementary Instruction (K–6)	Activities and Athletics
Junior High Instruction (7–8)	Building Operations and Maintenance
High School Instruction (9–12)	Business Services
Student Activities (Athletics and Co-Curricular)	Curriculum and Instruction
Summer School	Guidance/Counseling/Health Services
Vocational Education	Human Resources
Gifted and Talented Instruction	English as a Second Language
Special Education Instruction and Support	District Media and Technology
Instructional Support (Curriculum and Evaluation)	Music and Fine Arts
Instructional Media and Technology	Research, Evaluation, and Assessment
Instructional Delivery (Staff Development)	Districtwide Special Education
Pupil Support Services (Guidance, Counseling, Health, etc.)	Staff Development
Operations and Maintenance	Governance and Management
Sites, Buildings, and Improvements	Talented and Gifted Instruction
Transportation Services	Transportation Services
	Vocational Education
	Community Education
	Food Services

fund (maintenance and operations fund in some states). Programs that are usually not included are (1) those that are provided for with separate funds designated by the state or system, (2) enterprise or entrepreneurial programs that are entirely self-supporting, or (3) externally funded programs, such as federally supported programs.

It's important to note that some programs may have other, even multiple, revenue sources; but the programs may still be included if any portion of the general fund is consumed by the program. For example, athletic programs have gate receipts but require some general fund support. Many curricular and extracurricular programs have booster organizations that provide support, but additional funding comes from the system's general fund. Food service programs are usually enterprises with profits and losses, and they collect revenues from sales of food items; nevertheless, frequently the program requires support from the general fund. Each of these examples normally would be included in the performance-based budgeting process because of its linkage to the general fund of the system.

The determination to include or not include a program, of necessity, revolves around whether or not the program consumes funds from the system's main or general fund. If the program received some financial funding from the general fund, the program is competing for limited dollars with other programs. Consequently, the program needs to be a part of the priority-setting process and included in the program list for consideration in the process.

> NOTE: At this point in the process, the system is better positioned to undertake cost-benefit analyses. With the budget delineated in activity or program terms, the system has connected areas of program activity with actual expenditures. Both of these factors are necessary ingredients of a cost-benefit analytical process. Without the designation of program activities and connections to costs incurred or allocated, the system is unable to conduct cost-benefit analyses to see if results warrant expenditure levels previously experienced or to determine what value is obtained from the expenditures and allocations.

4. Addressing Other Preparation Requirements (SP + one and a half months)

Some of the other preparation requirements needing to be addressed by the administration include the following:

Determining Relationships to the System's Strategic or
Long-Range Planning Efforts (if relevant)

As explained earlier, a fully functioning and effective school system has little or no ambiguity about what the organization stands for or aims to achieve. If the aims and intentions of the system have been expressed in planning, those elements must be addressed and incorporated into the budget. In rational organizations, budgeting is a manifestation or product of the planning process, and it must be combined or blended together to assure organizational harmony and unity of purpose.

As Deming states, "Create constancy of purpose for continual improvement of products and service to society, allocating resources to provide for long range needs rather than only short term profitability, with a plan to become competitive, to stay in business, and to provide jobs" (Deming, 1986, pp. 23–24; 2000, p. 93).

Unless budgeting reflects planning already conducted and implemented, the system can fall into disunity and fragmentation.

Clarifying Lines of Responsibility

The organizational structure of the system identifies areas of responsibility, often meaning program management assignments, with corresponding programs, services, and activities. These assigned responsibilities and their relationships are instrumental and important to smooth coordination of effort and optimization of organizational functions and operations. Diversification of functions in the organizational structure needs to be in harmony to effectuate and accomplish the organizational mission. In the budgeting process, synchronization between educational factors and financial factors is essential, and both dimensions must work together to meet the priority needs of the system. The organizational structure must foster synchronization and fluidity of management against common goals and objectives or face the possibility of fragmentation and ineffectual action.

Ascertaining Enrollment Trends and Characteristics of Client Success

One of the tautologies in educational research and planning is that no amount of information is enough for perfect decision making. That is, confronting the uncertainties of a system's future, it is obvious that if information were perfectly complete, decisions would be seamless and unequivocally precise.

Regrettably, education is replete with challenges without complete and entirely adequate information to use in addressing those challenges. As a result, the practitioner must make aggressive efforts to obtain as much information about matters affecting the organization's direction, needs, and effectiveness.

The trends in enrollment are critical in predicting the demographic and sustenance requirements for the system's financial allocations. Not only are the expectations for enrollment in future years important, but the nature and characteristics of the clientele are important as well. Without adequate knowledge and understanding of the clientele and their individual needs, system planning is tenuous and allocations are vulnerable to error.

Building a Shared Foundation of Financial Information

Performance-based budgeting is not intended to be a closely held decision-making process, which has often characterized budget planning in the past. Some of the information that needs to be transparent and shared openly with the system's constituency includes the following:

- Clarification of the fund structure of the system
  - Tax capacities, rates, and restrictions
  - Costs per student and differentiated student costs by category (e.g., special education, English language learning, poverty classifications, etc.)
  - Definitions of all system funds and fund accounting structures

- Descriptions of revenue expectations
  - Revenue formulations and sources
  - Accurate enrollment projections supporting revenue
  - Estimations of revenue by source for current and future years

- History of expenditures and expenditure patterns over the past five years
  - Delineation of the cost of doing business by program or activity area

These miscellaneous preparation needs comprise essential information for joint and collaborative decision making as the process moves forward.

Connecting and Defining Program Categories With Increment Levels (SP + two months)

Program categories were addressed earlier; however, the administration needs to determine and prescribe the budgeting components within each program category included in the process. Not all program categories need to be included in the performance-based budgeting process, and in some special situations allocations may be omitted from the process. The following are some examples found in school systems over the past decade where categories are "outside" the process. They include situations when the administration or governing body has decided to set some budget program areas in place without inclusion in the prioritization process.

- Payment of an adjudicated judgment or legal settlement (single occasion)
- Large single expenditures occurring only one time (i.e., a catch-up investment in technology upgrades)
- Inflationary adjustments, salary reserve, or union agreement costs
- Investment in a sinking fund to pay off debt

Excluded costs are not frequently used in the process, probably because they are often interpreted as arbitrary, imposed without full evaluation, and preemptive of more rational, inclusive decision-making processes. Nevertheless, they are occasionally found in some systems.

Defining Components or Increment Levels

Each program is usually required to have at least three levels of budgeting in the performance-based budgeting process, which usually manifests the following components or increments:

- A "recovery" level of funding increment—meaning a reduction in funding from the previous year, thereby providing the system with a way to recover previously allocated funding
- The current or existing level of funding increment—meaning the same funding as the previous year, with or without an inflationary adjustment

- An "enhancement" level of funding increment—meaning an increase of funding in real terms to expand programs and services or improve the level of quality with additional funding

Of course, the recovery and enhancement levels may have two or more components each. One school system in Montana used five levels of recovery, starting at 75% of the prior year, and increasing amounts by 5% up to the 95% level. Some systems have left the enhancement levels unlimited, allowing program managers to propose multiple levels of program funding for program expansion or improvement. One school district in Iowa actually funded a technology program enhancement component with a 322% increase over the prior, which was designated to provide pronounced improvement in the hardware and software for student classrooms in order to "catch up" with surrounding school systems.

Recovery Increment Level Determinations

Recovery increment level determinations are usually made on the basis of the estimated revenue shortfalls or inadequacies for the subsequent year, necessitating budget retrenchment or reductions in order to maintain alignment with available revenues. For example, the system estimates that it may lose 10% of its current funding level by state cutbacks or after adjusting for cost increases. It is not uncommon for a system to find that negotiated salary commitments or inflationary costs within a state-limited funding structure may reduce funds previously available, resulting in establishing a recovery point for increment levels.

As a rule of thumb, if a school system estimates that it will experience a 5% reversion or reduction of revenue, the system needs to start the recovery increment levels at *twice* that amount, or 10%. If the increment levels are within the 10% (such as a 90% level and a 95% level), it would be reasonable to speculate that no more than half of all program allocations would need a reduction of 10% to achieve alignment between expenditures and revenues. Also, the system might choose to establish recovery increment levels for all programs in 2% segments as shown in Exhibit 6.2.

There is no preferred or "magic" number of components or increments. Each system has to determine for itself how much funding needs to be recovered due to economic and financial constraints. Also, the system may use the process in conditions of system growth or expansion, with a greater set of add-on increments for system improvement or program enhancement.

Codification of Program Increments

As introduced in the previous section, a budget codification system is necessary to keep track of the increments within a program. For ease of reference, systems often use a locally-developed two- to four-digit code for each program and two- to three-digit code for each program component. For example, in Exhibit 6.3, elementary education and library and media services each may have five increments, and could be coded as shown there.

Exhibit 6.2   Example of Multiple Increments

Level Description	Amount of Increment or Component	Program Cumulative Total
Base Recovery Increment	90%	90%
1st Add-On Recovery Increment	2%	92%
2nd Add-On Recovery Increment	2%	94%
3rd Add-On Recovery Increment	2%	96%
4th Add-On Recovery Increment	2%	98%
Current/Existing Increment	2%	100%
1st Enhancement Increment	5%	105%
Additional Enhancement Increments	X%	10X%

Exhibit 6.3   Example: Codification of Program Increments

1110 (Elementary Education)

    1110-01 Base increment (90%)
    1110-02 Recovery increment (95%)
    1110-03 Current increment (100%)
    1110-04 Enhancement increment (105%)
    1110-05 Enhancement increment (110%)

2500 (Library and Media Services)

    2500-01 Base increment (90%)
    2500-02 Recovery increment (95%)
    2500-03 Current increment (100%)
    2500-04 Enhancement increment (105%)
    2500-05 Enhancement increment (110%)

Note in the example above that the program code is four digits and the increment packages are each two digits. It's also important to note that the increments move in 5% amounts, but that was for illustration only. Some increments may be as little as 1% or as large as 300%. However they are structured, after the base increment, the additional amounts are increments only, *not* cumulative totals of the amount budgeted at that point. For example, the recovery increment in Exhibit 6.3 is stated as 95%, but in actuality it is only a 5% increment, to be added to the previous increments in order to make the 95% level. Similarly, each increment is only a 5% increase, to be added to the previous base and increments if funded.

Of course, if funded, the activities funded by that incremental component would commence and be implemented. As each increment is approved for funding, the activities embedded in the increments become funded and operational.

Advantages of Recovery Increments or Components

It is recommended that systems always use at least a minimal number of recovery increments or components because it is frequently inappropriate to assume that previous funding levels for programs and services continue to be sound and valid. Experience has shown that allocation decisions over time may have a limited life span in terms of necessity, making it prudent to re-examine previous allocations in light of current conditions or needs.

For example, one program may receive budgeted funds in a given year to acquire needed file cabinets for student records. Once procured, the funds allocated to that school might need to be recovered by the system because the cabinets have been purchased and the funds are no longer needed in that program. However, if the system builds annual budgets based upon previous budget levels without re-evaluating the appropriateness of the previous amount, the funds for the file cabinets would reappear in the school's budget without a specific end use or need. Budgets grow over time, and automatic, across-the-board increases may or may not be justifiable when examining the specific needs of programs within the system.

The use of recovery increments or components in performance-based budgeting reduces the possibility of redundant funding for activities or matériel from year to year by reevaluating prior year allocations against current or future needs.

Building the Decision-Making Budget
Advisory Team (SP + two months and one week)

Deciding who should sit at the table for budget deliberations, including ranking of program priorities, requires consideration of several factors. One consideration involves deciding who should serve, but another consideration is deciding who *should not* sit at the budget deliberations table. For example, the superintendent and members of the governing board should not participate in the planning sessions for obvious reasons—they comprise the body that will receive the recommendation from the budget-planning team, and several problems arise if they in fact sit as members of the recommending body.

These problems include the following:

1. Perhaps a board member's greatest asset as a community representative is his or her capacity to apply dispassionate, objective judgment on decisions and problems confronting the system. Indeed, a board member or superintendent has a professional and ethical duty to exercise his or her professional judgment without bias or self-interest. Participating in the decisions to recommend to their board places board members in the potential position of introducing personal bias in decisions.

2. Moreover, their voices are not without undue influence to the group. For example, superintendents and board members are often perceived by subordinate members of the organization as powerful. The perceived authority creates a greater/lesser relationship which may have a chilling effect on the objectivity and forthright contributions of subordinates (Poston, 1994).

3. Finally, board member participation in system committees, other than sub-committees of the board itself, frequently results in politicization of matters which come before the system, including financial allocations. Although individual members of boards ostensibly have no authority unless meeting as a total board, the "collective voice" of the board may become fractured or fragmented if individual members of the board encroach on the budget planning team's functions, activities, and deliberations.

Consequently, it is generally not considered a good idea to have superintendents or board members participating as members of the budget advisory team; however, meetings of the budget advisory team normally are open to the public and spectators may attend and observe deliberations. In such cases, it should be pointed out that the advisory team is a planning group meeting in public, not a public meeting in which anyone and everyone might participate. Limiting active participation in the sessions to the legitimate members of the advisory group prevents politicization of the process or instances of pressure tactics applied to the team's meetings.

Selecting Members for the Budget Advisory Team

Within the system and community, there are a number of stakeholders that might be included in the budget planning deliberations, including the following prospective participants:

- *Program managers.* The individuals who supervise and manage programs and services within the system are critical members of the budget planning team. The program managers plan, organize, deploy, implement, and administer the program; and their voice in resource allocations is the most credible and valid source of information about their program or service to the team. Each program defined for inclusion in the performance-based budgeting system needs to have an appointed manager that is in charge of the program from initiation to completion. Most program managers have systemwide or central responsibilities. However, some managers may supervise more than one program or service, so the number of budget-planning team members may actually be less than the number of programs. In any case, this membership component usually has fifteen to twenty individuals serving on the budget team.
- *Major central administrators.* The central administrators with broader, conceptual responsibilities for system management are also essential members of the budget planning team. Generally, this includes the chief academic officer, the chief financial officer, the human resources administrator, and occasionally a designated financial accounting official. Since the main

mission of a school system centers on pupil learning, it is recommended that the budget planning team meetings be chaired by the chief academic officer. The chief financial officer will usually have plenty to do just keeping track of financial factors and decisions.

- *Principals.* Not all principals in the system need to participate unless the system is a very small organization, but principals from at least two elementary schools, one middle school, and one high school need to be on the team. Without them, the integrity and credibility of information about program implementation needs at the school level would be jeopardized. The principals may serve as the representatives of their counterparts and may also double as program managers for school-based programs and components (i.e., instruction, principal's office, etc.).

- *Teachers.* Teachers are the custodians of the main mission for the school system, and their participation is very important to establish validity of information about program design, delivery, and outcomes. Teachers are line officers in the system's organization, and at least four teachers need to be on the budget team—one elementary, one middle school, one high school, and one special program teacher. In some systems, the assignment of teachers to system committees is the responsibility of the teachers' organization, and in other systems, it is the responsibility of the administration. Regardless of how they are appointed, teachers comprise a highly significant part of the decision-making body. The teachers' participation provides key perspectives on system classroom operations not available elsewhere in the system.

- *Support personnel.* Representatives from major support areas for teaching and learning need to be involved in the budget deliberations as well. Generally, this includes representatives from support functions that are underwritten with resources from the general operating fund, such as transportation, secretarial or clerical, custodial, maintenance, and food service operations.

- *Parents.* The addition of parent representatives to the budget planning team greatly increases the integrity of the process by obtaining critical information from "customers" of the system. The perspective of system clientele comes from a unique point of view—from the service delivery point and the end user of the system's programs and services. Parents need to be equal in number to the number of teachers on the team. If there are four teachers, there should be four parents as well.

- *Patrons.* Residents of the system, who do *not* have children in schools, need to participate in the budget planning for their schools. Patrons, with no children in school, comprise about 61% of the community (Bushaw & McNee, 2009). That noticeably large group comprises a key constituency—one which provides financial support to the public school system—and their voice must be heard as well. One school system in Ohio not only invited patrons (equal in number to parents) to participate in their budget planning process, but the superintendent also contacted the local chamber of commerce and requested that the chamber appoint a member to participate in the budgeting process. The business representative became one of the staunchest supporters of the local public school system and was a very important member of the budget planning process.

- *Students.* Of course, this is an optional addition to the budget team, but some school districts have had good success with high school student leaders participating in the budget planning process. One district used the student body presidents of each of its two high schools to participate on the budget team, and reports indicated that it was a good decision.

To a great extent, the composition of the membership of the budget planning team lies within the discretion of the superintendent and school board policy. Regardless of who the members of the team are, it is very important to provide each budget team participant equal opportunities for expression of ideas, responses to questions, and an equal vote to other members of the team when priorities are determined.

In effect, the budget planning team is a "one person—one vote" organization, and each participant shares all the benefits and responsibilities as any other member of the budget team.

Structuring and Organizing the Budget Advisory Team

The budget advisory team, once configured, will need leadership and structure to function effectively. Some key functions requiring attention include the following:

- *Scheduling.* Responsibility for planning, setting, and disseminating the meetings schedule must be assigned. School systems use different approaches to scheduling, with some using mostly evening sessions, some using Saturday sessions, and some using sessions during the normal work day. The latter approach may require substitutes for teachers, bus drivers, and others. The following events normally are expected:
  - Training in program component preparation requirements (scope, mechanics, etc.)
  - Verification of authorization to proceed from the superintendent or board
  - Program manager training and assignments relative to how to prepare program incremental components
  - Communication of timelines for development of program component packages
    - ➤ Content expectations
    - ➤ Deadlines and rules
  - Training in the component ranking strategies and nominal group techniques
  - Final presentations of program components
  - Following board procedures and approval requirements

- *Timing.* Time limits for advisory team sessions have proven to facilitate more expeditious meetings and to prevent excessively drawn-out sessions.
- *Presiding.* The duties of chairing the group and presiding over the sessions typically are assigned to the chief academic officer. The chair calls the

meeting to order, maintains parliamentary discipline within the group, recognizes speakers, and in general moves the meeting along.

- *Presenting.* Program managers have the responsibility for preparing budget proposals in accordance with the incremental components established by the system, presenting them to the budget advisory team within the established procedures, answering questions from team members, and serving as a resource and advocate for a given program and its subunits.
- *Providing data.* The chief financial officer is usually responsible for aggregating all costs inclusive of program components, preparing documentation of the financial data, and providing that information to members of the advisory team. Often the data are in line-item or function-object codification formats, which require all or part of a given line-item object code to be assigned to an appropriate program.
  - o Object codification is maintained for all item costs included in program components, so the performance-based budget may be translated later back into the required budget format used by the system or state. In any case, financial information must be accurate, openly accessible, and identified for each program component.
  - o Financial information is needed by the advisory team:
    - ➤ Descriptions and explanations of the system's financial framework and funds (see Exhibit 6.4)
    - ➤ Restrictions and limitations on fund uses (i.e., student activity funds may not be expropriated for the system's general fund)
    - ➤ Activities designated for each program area and its components
    - ➤ Budget component packaging, nomenclature, and inclusions
    - ➤ Definitions and procedures for cost-benefit analysis
    - ➤ Financial information accountability requirements

It is important that comprehensive financial information (see again Exhibit 6.4) is provided to budget advisory team members so that all participants have equal access to how the financial system works and the nature of terminology used. Participatory decision making is strengthened when all members of the decision-making body are equally informed and knowledgeable, and greater likelihood of success is assured.

In the Exhibit 6.4, the Minnesota school district made every effort to inform the members of its budgeting team as to basic financial information for school systems in that state. This type of information greatly improves the chances of the team's coherence and collaboration in the decision-making process.

Building the Performance Based Incremental
Units (Packages) (SP + four months)

This phase of constructing the performance-based budget takes considerable time, extending the time lime from the starting point nearly an additional two months, making the amount of time scheduled at this point to be four months. It may

Exhibit 6.4 Sample Fund Structure Information

(Minnesota School District)

General Fund (74.3% of Total Budget)

The general fund includes all of the annual operating costs (primarily salaries and employee benefits). The primary source of funding is the state formula allowance per pupil unit, the excess levy referendum and certain categorical state and federal grant programs. Except for the grant programs, there is no restriction on the use of general fund revenues.

Food Service Fund (3.9% of Total Budget)

The food service program is entirely supported by ticket sales and Federal reimbursements. Federal requirements prohibit the transfer of any excess resources out of the food service fund.

Transportation Fund (4.7% of Total Budget)

The transportation fund includes all of the costs of providing transportation services to students. The district is allowed $170 per pupil unit in the form of levy and aid. Since this is part of the funding formula and has been folded into the general fund, the state does not restrict how we can spend the $170. Hence, any reductions in our existing transportation services can be used to help our general fund.

Community Service Fund (3.3% of Total Budget)

The Kidstop childcare program is entirely self-supporting through fee revenue. All other programming is funded by State categorical revenue and supplemented by fees. State rules prohibit districts from transferring revenues out of the community service fund.

Capital Expenditure Fund (6.5% of Total Budget)

The capital expenditure fund includes the leasing, alteration, and upgrading of buildings, in addition to the purchasing of furniture, equipment, technology, textbooks, and library books. This fund has also been folded into the general fund. However, all operating capital, health/safety, and disabled accessibility categorical revenue can only be used for capital items.

Debt Service Fund (7.3% of Total Budget)

Revenue for this fund consists entirely of the levy and state aid required for debt payments on outstanding bonds. State law prohibits using these revenues for any other purpose.

NOTE: There are three other separate funds that are designated for specific purposes and not usually considered as part of the regular budget:

New Building Fund – Used only when a district has passed a bond to build a new facility.

Internal Service Fund – Used to fund the district's severance benefit liability.

Trust & Agency Fund – Used to account for gifts to the district.

take quite a bit of time to convert from the previous budget format to the activity-centered, performance-based approach with increments, often referred to as "packages."

Program managers are assigned the lion's share of responsibility for organizing their program's increment packages, apportioning resources across the range of packages, and involving key personnel in developing program features and options.

At this point in the process, the budget level increments, expressed as percentage maximums of the previous year's budget, will be established for the budget year. This configuration may look something like the example in Exhibit 6.5.

Exhibit 6.5   Example of Program Increment Packages

Program Code (xxxx)

xxxx-01   Base increment (90%)

xxxx-02   Recovery increment (95%)

xxxx-03   Current increment (100%)

xxxx-04   Enhancement increment (105%)

xxxx-05   Enhancement increment (110%)

The program increment package levels are usually established by the superintendent or superintendent's designee, and each program manager is charged with the responsibility to prepare a program package for each of the increments. Normally, enhancement increments are not limited in number; but that determination is within the discretion of the superintendent. That allows improvement in some areas and activities of the system, while simultaneously, reduction of services or activities might be occurring elsewhere in the system.

Other than developing the program packages, program managers often are advised or required to work with appropriate staff in the preparation of the packages. For example, the director of athletics might be developing program packages and activity delivery proposals for the activities-athletics program, and such development would be facilitated by participation of coaches and sponsors in designing incremental components and packages.

Program Manager Responsibilities

Program managers normally work with staff members and parents/patrons to develop the appropriate number of program increment packages. The leadership responsibilities for accomplishing this task would include, but not necessarily be limited to, the following tasks:

1. Organize and convene the program planning team, including staff and parents/patrons:
   a. Establish meeting agenda(s)
   b. Suggested agenda for first meeting:
      i. Introductions
      ii. Overview of the process
      iii. Review of resource materials

    iv. Review of forms to be used

    v. Establishment of team meetings schedule (times and dates)

    vi. Assignment of duties (recording and reporting minutes, providing refreshments, etc.)

    vii. Beginning review of the program area

2. Keep participants informed of meetings with reminders, advanced copies of agenda, and distribution of minutes for all sessions

3. Preside over meetings and help proceedings by facilitating staying on task, meeting timelines, aiding participant comfort, and distributing minutes

4. Obtain and maintain data resources for group use as needed, and find answers or data in response to individual participants' questions

5. Maintain linkage with the financial services department

6. Arrange for the printing, reporting, and presenting of program increment packages to the budget advisory team:

    a. Develop beforehand the intended purpose and objectives of the program and the methodology for evaluating results

    b. Assure that all program increment requirements are met accurately and appropriately

    c. Provide all information as needed to the budget advisory team in regard to the individual program and its parts

---

Leadership is always a key ingredient of organizational success, and the leadership of the program manager is no less important in the program area team's work in designing and preparing budget packages. In the program area, the program manager is the leader who has full responsibility for success of the team in accomplishing its work.

SUMMARY

In this chapter, the tasks to be completed and the time line to be followed have been presented. The schedule of events clarifies what needs to be accomplished and when. The increment levels need to be defined, and the advisory team identified and configured. Once the budget advisory team is configured and the program managers have been vested with their duties and responsibilities, the process for constructing the performance-based budget is in place; and the system is ready to implement budget increment package development under the leadership of program managers. The next chapter explains the specifics of package design and development.

7

Developing Performance-Based Budget Increment Packages

One business manager reported that he budgets for schools by "letting principals know how much they may have." This is emblematic of a "closely held" budgeting system. On the other hand, systems with performance-based budgeting ask principals, "What do you need to do to improve learning at your school?" or "What do you need to accomplish, what will it take, and how will you know if you're successful?"

The components of a performance-based budget are incremental subunits within a program activity budget with discernable purposes, methodologies, costs, and anticipated results. The increments build upon one another starting from a minimum funding level and proceeding to enhancement levels of funding with greater quality and cost. In the previous chapter, the process was described in terms to permit organizing deployment to prepare for the initiation of the process. This chapter provides specific guidance about how to design and build budgeting increment packages within an individual program.

PROGRAM MANAGER PROCEDURES FOR PREPARING BUDGET PACKAGES

There are specific steps for developing and preparing program increments or packages. Some of the key steps of program package development, which are helpful to program managers and staff, include the following activities and processes:

1. Review the district mission, objectives, strategies, and expectations and examine historical program costs and budget data. Build connections between program activities and system goals.

2. Accumulate and evaluate information about program status, performance, quality, and met and unmet clientele needs in recent years.

3. Consider how the methods, means, and delivery of this program unit relate with overall school system or clientele needs.
   o Ask the question: To what extent is this activity/program/service necessary or justifiable?
   o Analyze alternative methods of performing the functions of the program.
   o What other ways are there to accomplish this function?
   o Are other ways better? Less expensive? Provide additional benefits?
   o What different levels of services and costs are possible?
   o What impact would various alternatives have on other programs and activities?

Note that the most critical elements in evaluating alternatives include consideration of the following issues with suggested questions to be asked.

4. Different ways of performing the function need describing:
   o What types of different methodologies or technologies are there?
   o Which is more cost-effective—in-house or outsourcing?
   o Which are better—centralized functions or decentralized functions?

5. Different levels of effort for performing the function need defining:
   o What is the minimum level possible below current operating level?
   o What additional levels of activity might be added as funding increases?

6. Efficacy or performance of a given program component needs assessing:
   o How will the performance of a given program component be defined?
   o How will people know if the purpose of the program component is achieved?

7. Program managers need to confer with directors, coordinators, supervisors, business managers, principals, teachers, and others who may have an interest in the activity or who can provide useful information about program alternatives.

8. A package for each level of funding needs to be prepared. (Note: The enhancement levels are optional.)

In constructing budget incremental packages, the minimum program level (i.e., 90%) may not completely achieve the total operational requirements of the program or activity, but it needs to be a fully operational program that will function at a lower cost and probably a lower level of quality.

Adjusting Program Activities and Operations to Funding Oscillations

As funding availability ebbs and flows in public education, it is often agonizing for educators to consider reductions of service to students and learners or changes in the allocations for employee groups. However, school systems are highly labor-intensive organizations, and flexibility for modifying costs is in short supply. Many school systems' total budgets are actually 90% or more committed to staffing and employee salaries and benefits. With that designated use, the opportunity to find "slack" is very constricted.

Nonetheless, in cases where retrenchment is called for, something has to give. It may be that program managers choose to address the most critical populations being served by programs or the most serious areas of need and limit service to less-critical clients. It goes without saying that the minimum package funding levels in all probability would reduce the current level of service provided. However, the minimum package might also reflect operating improvements, organizational changes, or improvements in efficiency that result in cost reductions. Many such options have been successful.

For example, one system changed the mode of delivery of custodial services from in-house operations to an outsourced option at considerable savings. Another system collaborated with neighboring school systems to form a cooperative insurance organization to reduce employee benefit costs. However, not all options are improvements. For example, one system modified its library services program in its elementary schools from a professional librarian model to a para-professional clerk model. Obviously, the quality of service from the professionally trained librarian model would be expected to be superior to the lesser alternative.

The Option of Modifying Allocations at the School Site

One of the least popular, but perhaps one of the most practical, options is to consider resource allocation modifications at the school building itself. An aversion to changing allocations that impact personnel is understandable, but it may be only a psychological constraint due to the fact that often as much as 80% of the system budget is spent at the school sites (Odden & Archibald, 2001).

Considering that the lion's share of school district funding goes to instructional activities and programs at school buildings, and considering also that with instructional activities, the majority of funds translate into personnel expenditures, then instructional expenditures must be at issue. In many school systems, there simply may be precious little to consider for modification outside of personnel allocations.

In times of scarcity and economic distress, resources become harder to come by. Resource reallocations may emerge to become the chief vehicle for a school system to realize its educational vision. In other words, money to improve performance and student learning may have to come from money the system already has. Funding for new (and best) practices can conceivably come from funding for existing, perhaps less than effective, practices. Unconventional thinking and creativity in use of available funds, including personnel utilization, is needed to move toward performance and productivity improvement.

The Option of Abandonment

Abandonment is the ultimate option for consideration of program component budgeting. For example, imagine that the system has provided a particular type of service for a considerable number of years. If funding were to be diminished, the service level naturally would have to be reduced. One district in Iowa spends over $2 million annually for transporting all of its 6,000-plus students. If the money were not available, some students obviously might have to find other means for getting to school. Policy decisions like this have the opportunity for a strong and tangible connection between funds available and the quality of service. Without the funding, the service is "abandoned."

While this sounds harsh and unpleasant to just leave something out, the practice is abundantly found in the social culture. For example, when shopping at a grocery store, renting an apartment, or purchasing an automobile, it is routinely expected that payment is required before acquisition of the desired item. Without payment, there are neither groceries, nor apartment, nor automobile.

It is often said that schools are asked to do too much (Editorial, 2003). A plethora of initiatives is frequently confronting school administrators, and time and resources are simply not sufficient to provide for accomplishment of the countless expectations for public schools. Given a typical 180 school days with approximately 5 hours per day of instructional time, the school year contains only about 1,000 hours with which to work. If there are six or more content areas to be addressed, the typical school course/program has only about 166 hours per year to use in accomplishing its purposes. It comes as no surprise that with limited time and limited resources, unlimited expectations are out of the question. Something plainly needs to be left out. How to make that decision is another matter altogether.

Aligning Resource Allocations to Program Needs

One approach for budgeting is to link what the organization needs to accomplish with what resources the organization will require to reach that accomplishment. By connecting objectives or activities in programs to funding resources, the relationship clearly speaks to the essentiality of each requiring the other. Without the funding, the objective cannot be met. For example, if a high school counseling program needs to reduce counselor–student ratios to improve service, funding for an additional position would normally be needed. However, if funding is not provided, the additional staffing is not provided; and the objective to reduce counseling loads has to be abandoned accordingly.

The lack of clear understanding of the difference between what the funding "is" as opposed to what the funding "does" is not uncommon in many parts of the United States.

Given this conundrum, it's very important to remember that one of the goals of performance-based budgeting is to connect costs to quality in a very tangible manner, so policy makers and decision makers in education can readily see the value of different levels of service in unambiguous and beneficial terms. It is only reasonable to assume that given appropriate information about needs, communities generally would opt for quality and high performance in their public schools.

Whatever a community can do for some of its children, it needs to do for all of its children (Dewey, 1916). The information the community needs to make such commitments and to provide such opportunities emanates, in part, from clearly seeing the relationship between money spent and results obtained.

Accordingly, two things are needed for each program increment package. Each package (subunit or component) needs to (1) stand alone and operate at each designated level of funding and (2) show clear and observable connections between what might be spent and what might be obtained or achieved.

Financial information may actually be less convincing than program quality information. For example, if there were two packages in an instrumental music program—one at 90% of current cost and the other at current cost, which provides for instrumental music instruction to begin in the schools at fourth grade. The lesser-cost package might well reduce the level of quality—calling for instrumental music instruction to start at the sixth grade instead of fourth grade. When conceptualized and stated in this manner, the discussion and considerations usually focus more on the type and quality of service than on the actual costs involved between the two alternatives.

It's critical for creative program delivery planners to "think outside the box" by imagining different ways and means for accomplishing the purposes of a program at different funding levels. Creative thinkers recognize that the way things are may not be the way they need to be.

PERFORMANCE-BASED BUDGETING PACKAGE DESCRIPTIONS AND PARTS

Program packages are comprised of the budget requests for a given program at a specific funding level. A program package will be prepared for each of the designated funding increment levels. Program managers, working with appropriate staff, analyze their programs and develop a series of budget requests that cumulatively represent the total program package.

In each program package, the purposes and fiscal requirements of a program's funding level are detailed. In an attempt to standardize the format and information as an aid to the advisory team in decision making, each program package should contain the following:

- A title that communicates the program, the level, and the nature of the package
- A clear statement of purpose that details the nature of what is to be accomplished
- Estimated cost and benefit of the activity or program level
- Consequences of funding or not funding the activity or program level
- Methods for evaluating the performance, accomplishments, or efficacy of a given program increment or component

Since each package specifies just what will be accomplished by its funding level, the budget advisory team, superintendent, and board will know just exactly what is being gained or lost when a particular package is approved or disapproved for inclusion in the funded budget plan.

Fiscal data for the planning and preparing of program packages will be prepared by the business office. The business manager will be the resource person for all financial data. Final packages will also contain a chart of accounts and all necessary information for translating the performance-based budget into the state's line-item reporting format.

Exhibit 7.1 provides a sample form that shows the information provided by the program managers and used by the budget advisory team in its deliberations.

Exhibit 7.1   Sample School System Budget Package Description Form

---

Performance-Based Budget Package Description

Unit/Package Title: _____

Package ID Code: _____   Package Cost: _____

Prepare a separate description on this form for each program component or increment.
Please confine information to this form. Do not use attachments or additional pages.

1. Describe program activities and services provided by this package:

2. Describe how activities requested in this package will differ from the previous year's operation:

3. Describe how the package, if funded, will relate to or support established system goals and strategic plan:

4. Describe methods/means for assessment of the ends or accomplishments of this package:

5. What organizational results or outcomes will be affected if this package is NOT funded (also describe how):

Use of the form in Exhibit 7.1 requires the program manager to *briefly* state responses to the requested information. Many school systems require that the information be limited to one page for unique reasons. For instance, if the system had twenty-five programs with five funding levels each, that would equal 125 program components. Keeping track of that many variables in any decision-making process is no simple task. Use of brief, précis descriptions of program components facilitates a better conceptual view of all the individual funding requests. The budget advisory team's work is facilitated with summarizations of program components when rank ordering is to occur.

Compilations of all program component packages are also needed for the team to determine the overall budget component packages requested. A sample of the form listing all increment packages is found in Exhibit 7.2.

Exhibit 7.2 provides a quick and accurate grasp of the individual program packages that are requested for consideration of funding by each program manager. The information helps members of the budget advisory team (and superintendent and board) see which program packages are requested and what they cost.

The number of rows needs to equal the number of incremental packages authorized. For example, if there are five levels of funding called for (i.e., two recovery packages, one current package, and two enhancement packages), then the number of rows would be five. Each row represents the increment package description (fifty words or less), program manager name, program title, program identification code, total funding request, and a list of increment/packages. The

Exhibit 7.2   Sample Performance-Based Budget Unit Package List

Program Unit Increment Package List (Program Overview)

Prepare one of these forms for each program. List program components (increments) below.

Performance-Based Budget Unit/Program: _____

Manager: _____ Program ID Code: _____

Package List by Code	Increment/Package Titles	FTE	Package Cost

Total of Performance-Based Budget Unit/Program Requests: FTE $

Description of overall performance-based budget unit program (describe the purpose and nature of this program in fewer than 50 words):

list of packages also calls for each program increment/package's code, title, personnel positions (full-time equivalents), and cost.

All program managers use the same form and follow the same procedures in completing the form. Once each program increment or package has been described on the list, a third form which delineates all object code information for each package is needed. Exhibit 7.3 shows a sample form for this purpose.

In Exhibit 7.3, all of the budget items for an individual package are listed by object code. Of course, the object code is the specific cost item in accordance with the individual state or province's financial accounting system. This information is needed for the financial management officer to convert the performance-based budget back into line-item format (or any other format) required for financial account reporting and final budget compilation.

For example, if the program is elementary instruction, and the base package includes salaries for teachers, a couple of the object code items might be listed something like the example in Exhibit 7.4.

In the same way, every line item in the program increment/package would be listed with its corresponding object code, the FTE (full-time equivalents) of personnel, and the total amount with that object code. Once all program package

Exhibit 7.3 Sample Budget Package Cost Analysis Form

Unit/Package Title: _____

Package ID Code: _____   Total Cost: $_____

Prepare one of these forms for each program component or increment.

Object Description	Object Code	FTE	Amount
TOTAL:		**FTE**	**$**

Note: Add as many rows as needed.

Exhibit 7.4   Sample Object Code Designations

Object Description	Object Code	FTE	Amount
Teacher Salaries	110	17.5	$ 740,530
Employee Benefits	210	N/A	$ 211,051

object codes are tabulated, the performance-based system is structured for ease of exportation or conversion to other format configurations accordingly.

Budget Preparation Guidelines

Budget level constraints, expressed as percentage maximums of the previous year's budget, need to be established for the budget year as follows:

Minimum level	≤90%
Economy level	95%
Current level	100%
Current adjusted for inflation	104%
Growth level	≥104%

Each program unit manager will prepare budget packages, which if funded, would fall within these limits; and the budget unit manager will be the final authority as to budget unit contents and order of priority within a program. Each package will be given a code number, which shall be comprised of the program function designator as listed in this packet. The levels shall be coded as follows:

Minimum level	00
Economy level	01
Current level	02
Current adjusted	03
Growth level	04

For example, a given program is assigned a code (i.e., music and fine arts may be assigned a program designator code of T). If the program is comprised of three levels, each program component would be designated as listed below:

Minimum level	T-00
Economy level	T-01
Current level	T-02
Current adjusted	T-03
Growth level	T-04

Rank ordering of all packages across program areas or across budget units will be prepared by the budget advisory team (see next chapter for procedures).

FACTORS TO CONSIDER IN FABRICATING PROGRAM INCREMENT/PACKAGES

When constructing packages for specific programs, there are some issues that merit consideration by program managers. These factors include the following:

- Authenticity of resource allocations with activities
- Equity in program design and delivery
- Differential needs of learners
- Asymmetrical employee compensation

Each of these factors will be described in terms of its relationship to program increment packaging.

Authenticity of Resource Allocations With Activities

There is often skepticism about budget proposals in school systems. Occasionally, individuals who have submitted budget requests in the past exaggerate the resources required. This might be more political in nature than necessary in regard to structuring budget requests. The validity of funding is absolutely vital for gaining the economic confidence of the public school community, so resource requests need to be authentic. This means that the amount of money requested is derived from an explicit analysis of what (1) needs to be spent in order to perform a given service or reach an intended outcome, (2) can be documented completely as to validity of need, and (3) can be identified according to a carefully planned body of what is considered necessary for the need to be met adequately.

Inflating costs, overstating resources required, or misrepresentations of data are disingenuous at best, and detrimental to the integrity of the budgeting process. Politicization of budget requests is something to be avoided. Past resource allocations need careful scrutiny for accuracy and validity for meeting the program's needs. It is critical that resource allocation requests be trustworthy, verifiable, and essential in terms of what it really will take to accomplish the intended activity or perform the planned service.

Equity in Program Design and Delivery

Equity requires something different than equal treatment. Students are different and have different needs, and schools are different and have different needs. Different needs require different programs and services; but in designing programs, a factor that is often overlooked is the necessity for equity (Poston, 1992).

Equity remains a very serious problem in American schools. According to a study of school systems' spending patterns, current financial allocation systems allow for systemic biases against high-poverty schools. In this study, school systems examined were likely to distribute resources with the following imbalances and inequities (Roza & McCormick, 2006):

- Affluent schools are favored with more noncategorical dollars than poor schools.
- Teacher salary costs are unevenly distributed across schools with teachers in high-poverty schools paid at the lower end of the salary scale.
- In some cases, a portion of federal dollars is funneled disproportionately to affluent schools.
- High-poverty schools are shortchanged by subsidies to affluent schools to equalize and offset the federal and state dollars that are targeted for Title I schools.

The problems of equity persist in American schools, and the situation has implications for schools that are trying to gain equal success in learning by all students, rich or poor (Kozol, 1991). Distinguishing between equity and equality is a slippery slope. Equity is not the same as equality, but most often equal allocation systems comprise a substantial percentage of resource allocation systems. In *equality,* everything is equal. For example, resources for materials may be budgeted on a per-pupil basis, and a school would receive funding for supplies and materials in a given amount per pupil. In essence, the more pupils there are in the school, the more money there is in the school budget for materials and supplies. It may be equal, but it may also be unfair and discriminatory.

On the other hand, equity is characterized by justice or fairness and impartiality toward the school system's clientele. In reality, equity may manifest inequality of service for individual students or schools if reasonably based on individual student or school needs. In effect, if individual learner or school needs are dissimilar, equality may not be equitable for school systems. Public schools historically have sought to serve the needs of all learners, regardless of socioeconomic status, ethnicity, gender, religion, and so on. In performance-based budgeting, the goal of equity is valued, requiring a tighter nexus between resource allocation and individual learner and school needs.

Budget allocations are better driven by assessments of need rather than by enrollment or other quantitative factors (Downey, Steffy, Poston, & English, 2009). Resources by necessity need to flow disproportionately on the basis of need. For example, if one school in the system has a disproportionate number of students disadvantaged from poverty who demonstrate low achievement as a group, that school may need more personnel, supplies and materials, or facilities to meet the unique needs of that particular student population.

In the budgeting process, allocations on the basis of diagnosed, documented, and validated needs should be devised so as to be consistent with policy objectives of the school system (Caldwell, Levačić, & Ross, 1999). Naturally, this consideration may result in unequal allocations across schools, but the disproportional provision most likely will be regarded as equitable.

Differential Needs of Learners

For a program package to be *needs-based*, it must be constructed from a careful determination of what resources would be required to provide mastery of curriculum objectives for all students in specific school circumstances. The goal is for all students to achieve the specific objectives, while providing what it takes to assure equal success in schooling. Past allocation patterns may be inappropriate for this purpose.

Basic Core Program Allocation

At this point, costs for programs need to be calculated based upon per-student weighted factors (Abu-Duhou, Downes, & Levačić, 1999). Some of the factors to include in the calculation of basic allocations for the overall core program and clientele include the following:

- Number of students to be served by the program increment package
- Staffing requirements in accordance with the magnitude of needs to be addressed
- Support resources required for teaching and learning activities by program and grade level

Differentiated resources for individual student and/or school needs may be addressed after the average per-student cost for the program's teaching and learning needs has been determined. At this point, the customary needs across schools would be established; but additional costs for enrichment, remediation, special treatments, unique student factors, or school site features are not included (Duhou, Downes, & Levačić, 1999).

Differentiated Resource Allocations (weighting)

Differentiated resource allocations are then calculated based on the nature of students and schools that affect achievement and student success, such as socioeconomic disadvantage. Historically, educational institutions have been plagued with achievement gaps between economically advantaged student populations and disadvantaged student populations (English & Steffy, 2001). Other factors also require consideration to "level the playing field" for all students, as shown in Exhibit 7.5.

Exhibit 7.5 also delineates, major contributors to the identification of students' differential needs. While it is not a complete list, some consideration is needed when these factors are present in program design.

Weighting for age or grade level. Identified learning hindrances call for differentiated allocations of funds. Many school systems and governmental units have developed

Exhibit 7.5 Factors of Educational Need for Consideration in Funding

Factor	Description
Socioeconomic disadvantage (poverty)	Magnitude of poverty is a strong predictor of achievement deficits.
Incidence of low educational achievement	Proportions of "at risk" students have an effect on programmatic success.
Language fluency	Non-English speaking populations face difficulties in mastering learning objectives.
Acute learner difficulties and disabilities	Special needs often require individual resources and provisions for learner success.

weighted formulas for allocating funds based upon the needs and characteristics of the school clientele.

For example, in the United Kingdom, allocations per student are weighted for age as well as other factors (Levačić, 1999). In weighting, the structure of the funding formula for schools provides consideration for different ages (implicitly for different needs) of learners. Examples of the British weighting factors for age are shown in Exhibit 7.6.

In most U.S. states, school funding is differentially weighted by grade level. For example, in Arizona, the weights for students in kindergarten through eighth grade are 1.0, but the weights are 1.163 for high school students (Parrish, Harr, Anthony, Merickel, & Esra, 2003). The underlying rationale for this difference lies in the fact that high school students have broader and more comprehensive academic and matériel requirements that have higher aggregate costs than earlier grade levels.

Exhibit 7.6 Age-Weighted Allocations Per Student (United Kingdom 1997–1998)

Age	Ratio to Base
4–6	1.00
7–11	0.94
11–14	1.34
14–16	1.61
16–18	1.94

Weighting for socioeconomic factors. Other factors considered important to student-learning outcomes were examined in an Australian study, which determined that six factors were the best predictors of student achievement (Hill & Ross, 1999). The six factors in Australia included the following:

1. *Poverty.* Whether the student's family was receiving public assistance (such as free and reduced meals at school)

2. *Occupational status.* Whether the parent in the student's family was unemployed and categorized as unskilled, skilled, white collar, or professional in occupation

3. *Nonfluency in English.* Whether a language other than English was spoken at home

4. *Family composition.* Whether the student was living with one, two, or neither of his or her parents

5. *Aboriginality.* Whether or not the student identified himself or herself as an indigenous person (in the United States, this factor may relate to Native Americans, Alaskans, or Pacific Islanders)

6. *Transience.* Whether or not the student has recently changed schools

While a few of these factors are unique to Australia, there are similar counterparts in American schools. Factors frequently considered in budget allocations in the United States include the following:

- Incidence of eligibility for free and reduced school meals
- Nonfluency in English
- Native American status
- School mobility rates (student attrition and turnover)

Developing a means to weight these factors requires measurement of the impact upon student achievement by each factor. In the Australian study, five of the factors, except for *nonfluency in English*, were found to have identical impact upon achievement. The weighting for *nonfluency in English* was reduced by half to a 0.5 weight to prevent undue domination of the final factor (Hill & Ross, 1999).

In the state of Texas, weighting for socioeconomic factors was included in the state school-funding structure. Texas law provided that student enrollment counts (full-time equivalents) had weights as shown in Exhibit 7.7 (Clark & Toenjes, 1996).

Exhibit 7.7   Weighting for Special and Socioeconomic Factors (State of Texas 1995)

Special Program or Socioeconomic Status	Weighting Factor
Career and Technology Education	1.37
Gifted and Talented Programs	.12
English Fluency and Bilingual Education	.10
Compensatory Education (Free and Reduced Meals Eligible)	.20

In Texas, schools with students in the listed special programs or with socio-economic status equated with poverty receive additional funding on a per-student basis above and beyond the normal allocation.

Weighting for special educational needs. In the United States, each state chooses the system it will employ to provide additional funding for students with special educational needs. Some states use weights, block grants, census-related formulas, and other means. As an example of weights, the state of Arizona uses a multiple weighted pupil formula to distribute special education funds. The weights are added to the student base weight (1.0 for preschool and kindergarten through eighth-grade students, and 1.163 for high school students) and applied to the prior year's total student count to generate a weighted student count (Parrish et al., 2003).

The specific weights in the Arizona school-funding structure for special education are delineated in Exhibit 7.8.

In using the weights in Exhibit 7.8 if a school were to have a visually impaired student, the school would receive 4.832 times the basic per-student allocation at that grade level in Arizona.

Exhibit 7.8   Special Educational Needs Weighting (State of Arizona 1999–2000)

Special Education Need	Weight
Emotional Disability	0.003
Emotional Disability – Private	4.127
Hearing Impairment	3.341
Mild Mental Retardation	0.003
Moderate Mental Retardation	4.244
Multiple Disabilities With Severe Sensory Impairment	6.025
Multiple Disabilities/Autism/Severe Mental Retardation – Resource	4.235
Multiple Disabilities/Autism/Severe Mental Retardation – Self-Contained	5.015
Orthopedic Impairment – Resource	3.868
Orthopedic Impairment – Self-Contained	5.641
Other Health Impairment	0.003
Preschool – Severe Delay	4.979
Specific Learning Disability	0.003
Speech Language Impairment	0.003
Visual Impairment	4.832

Summary of weighting approaches. An obvious maxim is that students are different and schools are different. Some students have special educational needs, some have language or achievement issues, and others may require other types of special programs to meet their individual needs. Funding needs to respond to the different needs of students and schools, and the types of differences make a substantial list. The main thought to remember is that different characteristics of students and schools impact educational effectiveness; also, compensatory measures, including augmenting funding, need to be taken into account to overcome the hindrances to learning. In other words, funding needs to be unequal in order to be equitable and to level the playing field for all students.

Asymmetrical Employee Compensation

Staffing within schools has a strong impact upon funding. Staff and faculty training and longevity have long been considered in compensation policy and practice, creating an unbalanced distribution of payroll costs across schools. This unbalanced and disproportionate allocation practice is not desirable, and some method of handling this differential requirement by program managers is needed.

To resolve the problem in the performance-based budgeting system, personnel requirements are treated as numerical full-time equivalents, and each position is uniformly budgeted at an average cost per position for the system. If teachers at one school have annual salaries extending from $35,000 to $69,000 each, the problem is that the staff at another school will not be equal in number or in salary range. If the average teacher salary is $49,500, each school would budget that amount for each teaching position. In effect, the system prescribes an amount to budget for each position, which represents the average cost to the system for that type of position.

This will remedy the problem of disparate amounts per school for staffing and make staffing allocations more manageable in the budgeting deliberations. It is best to simply use an average salary for each and every position, whether it be for a teacher, principal, custodian, bus driver, and so on.

Once a budget is approved, individual schools need to have their specific budgeted personnel salaries reconciled with the actual salaries of their employees. The financial services department or the financial services officer normally assumes responsibility for reconciling budgeted positions with the actual salary amounts after the budget has been constructed using the average salary placeholder.

If the central office accepts this systemwide allocation responsibility, the practice prevents overfunding or underallocating for a specific school. For example, a school may have a teacher earning a salary of $72,000 who chooses to retire. If that amount money had been allocated in the budgeting process to the school, it is highly likely that it might create a "windfall" of extra funding for the school if the teacher's replacement is hired at a lower salary than that of the retiree.

The official policy of the system needs to be that positions, not actual dollars, will be budgeted for individual schools, and allocations made when the process is complete. Any salary reconciliation savings or additional costs must be a system responsibility. Savings on turnover, if left to the individual schools, might create a moral dilemma in which a school might conceivably seek to hire lower-paid, less-qualified staff members instead of more highly paid and qualified staff in order to obtain additional unallocated funds. This has not been an unknown circumstance in some school systems, and it has the likelihood of being detrimental to the quality of teaching and learning (Murnane & Phillips, 1981).

ASSEMBLING THE BUDGET PROPOSALS AND SETTING PRIORITIES

Once each program manager has completed construction and development of his or her program unit packages, with all required forms, the information is gathered from all program managers and assembled into a notebook (or similar binding) for the budget planning team to use in its deliberations. The book of program package proposals is typically voluminous. For example, if there are twenty programs and each has five packages, there will be 100 program packages in total with no fewer than two pages each and an additional page for the program—making a total of 220 pages or so. Obviously, there is much to absorb in the process of performance-based budgeting.

Some systems in this process use different colors of paper to facilitate ease of locating a package. For example, the program introduction page might be yellow, each package description form might be blue, and the object code tabulation for each package might be green.

The compiled budget package materials are then used in the budget-planning-team proceedings by all members of the group. The general process will be described in the next chapter.

SUMMARY

In this chapter, the process and procedures for program budget managers were delineated, and instructions were provided to guide program managers in preparing budget packages. Several considerations were discussed, including how to adjust program activities and operations to variable levels of funding, how abandonment works, and a description of the program package components and parts. Some factors to consider in package construction were discussed, which included factors of authenticity in aligning activities to allocation levels, assuring equity in program design and delivery, managing differential needs of learners with weighting approaches, and compensating for asymmetrical employee salaries and experience. The next step is to consolidate all program packages into an integral whole for the budget advisory team as they commence their work.

Determining Budget Priorities and Component Funding Levels

The Minneapolis school district conducted an audit of its educational programs in 2008. They were surprised to learn that the system had over 160 special program interventions implemented in their schools. One administrator referred to the proliferation of interventions as figuratively "jumping on the horse and riding off in all directions" to improve learning in schools. Fragmentation of program design, implementation, and assessment is not unlike a "shotgun" approach without focus. It goes without saying that some things are better than others, and resources aren't sufficient to be wasted on all widespread and uncoordinated efforts regardless of measured value.

BUDGET ORGANIZATION AND STATUS

At this point, program managers should have completed development of their program incremental packages and the budget for each program component package has been completed and prepared for dissemination. The next step is to assemble all programs with included packages into a document containing the unit increment package list (program overview) for each program (see Exhibit 7.2 in preceding chapter), followed by the program's budget package description forms—one for each package and established funding increment (see Exhibit 7.1 in preceding chapter), and the program's budget package cost analysis forms—one for each package (see Exhibit 7.3 in preceding chapter). With this commodious document in hand, the system's budget advisory team is ready to proceed with the development, organization, and priority setting of the performance-based budget.

BUDGET ADVISORY TEAM NEEDS

Before proceeding, members of the budget advisory team must be identified and assigned responsibility for collaboratively developing the budget and formulating the recommended budget for consideration by the system superintendent or chief executive officer. Each of the budget team members will need several things before they convene and commence their work, including the following:

- The compiled set of program managers' proposed budgets, with package information and forms required
- A document delineating the system's mission statement and goals
- A comprehensive list of all programs with all budget component packages organized by budget code or alphabetically
- Descriptive information and forms for each program package and components (package description forms)
- A calendar of the scheduled meetings of the budget advisory team and budgeting events (superintendent recommendation deadline, board meetings and presentations, etc.)
- Financial history of the system and revenue projections for the next budget year
- A list of members of the budget advisory team with position stated (teacher, parent, patron, etc.)

This type of information could be included in the budget advisory team's notebook for ease of access and transportability.

Considerations for Budget Advisory Team Meetings

Typical schedules for budget teams have ranged from three to nine meetings, each lasting two to three hours, with the average number of meetings occurring usually between three or four sessions. Some teams have chosen to meet in the evenings, which may extend the number of meetings. Other teams have met on a standard workday, with substitutes provided for teachers who are members of the team. The workday session may extend to several hours, but the number of sessions is greatly reduced. A few systems have conducted their meetings on Saturdays, with some stipend compensation for professional staff if necessitated by contractual obligations.

Normally, several sessions are scheduled within the available time frame, subject to rescission if the work of the budget advisory team is completed in fewer sessions.

Recommended Team Initial Discussion Points

It is important for the team to discuss and agree upon a few recommendations about the collaborative process in its inaugural session.

First, it is recommended that all members of the team have equal voting privileges when it comes to determining priorities among budget packages. One member, one vote, is the standard protocol.

Further, to support parity of all members of the team, it is recommended that the team meet in "round-table" fashion, with provision of ample table or desk space to work with materials and take notes. There are several simple ways to organize a meeting space with tables to accomplish this.

Also, participation by the superintendent (or CEO) or governing board members is strongly not recommended. This often creates dissonance and discord in discussions and injects unnecessary partiality, which distorts the decision-making functions of the team.

In addition, information about programs is recommended to be obtained solely from the program manager. The program manager is the spokesperson for the program. Each program exclusively determines whom the spokesperson for that program will be.[1] For reasons of efficacy in program management, the program manager must have final authority over his or her program.

Moreover, it is suggested that all members of the team need to provide assurance that they will participate fully in all sessions of the team. Absence for serious reasons may be unavoidable, but it is likely to prevent problems for the group if all parties are present during sessions.

Program managers may need to provide documentation about program development procedures. Some things of interest might include identifying who was involved in the program package development process, a description of how the program planning team made its decisions, and information about how the program's internal budget configuration was determined.

Inaugural Session Budget Advisory Team Tasks

In the initial session, it is important that budget advisory team members define and agree upon their tasks and responsibilities. Usually, the task is limited to listening, understanding, and discerning what is provided in program packages in terms of objectives, activities, costs, and anticipated results. The budget advisory team needs wide-ranging information to be effective, and some of the

---

[1] In some systems, the spokesperson has been a nonadministrative member of the staff for the program. For example, the spokesperson for the transportation program in one system was a bus driver (who was an excellent representative).

expectations for the initial meeting need to focus on the following issues and information.

- When programs and packages are presented to the team, it is critical for the relationship of each program to the school system's mission to be clearly understood.
- The team must seek to discern the effect of each program and package upon the system's activities and performance.
- The purpose of each program and its components must be clearly identified in terms of how success of the program will be determined.
- Methods and means for delivery of each program's activities and services need to be determined, including what options and alternatives were considered and/or presented.
- Each program package's budget, financial scope, and impact upon the financial standing of the system must be plainly illustrated and understood.

Members of the budget team also need to determine the schedule of meetings, location(s), and expectations for the sessions. For example, if the schedule includes early evening sessions, it's helpful to know if meal services or refreshments will be provided. Of course, other matters germane to the team's work may come up for discussion and decisions in this early session.

THE BUDGET TEAM PROCESS AND DELIBERATIONS

The budget advisory team will convene in accordance with its established schedule and calendar, and its main purpose is to review and examine all programs and budget packages sufficiently to gain insight and understanding of the ramifications of each component. Once the team has received presentations from program managers about each program package, the team will proceed in establishing priorities among the program packages.

In the process, program managers may be permitted by the team to withdraw a package, revise a package, or add a package in accordance with system needs at any point along the line of priority decision making.

Once packages are complete and presented to the team, the team will conduct a preliminary rank ordering of the packages, using nominal group techniques, explained later in this chapter. To begin the process of deliberation, it is advisable for the team to set some ground rules for the decision-making process.

Ground Rules for Budget Advisory Team Sessions

In meetings of the budget advisory team, the main activity is presentation of programs and their packages to the team by program managers or their designees. In order to make this process trouble free, ground rules for the team sessions are needed.

Chair Designation and Role

A chairperson is needed to preside over team meetings, to facilitate presentations by program managers, and to manage all sessions in general. Chairpersons may be appointed by the superintendent (or CEO) or be elected by the team according to policy of the system. A key preliminary task for the chair is to make all members of the team feel comfortable with one another and the work which lies ahead. Informality is preferable, but sound group management, or parliamentary, procedures are essential.

Typically, the chair does not vote, but this may be permissible if authorized by the team. Some systems use an outside person to chair their team meetings—that is, someone who is independent of the system's operations and functions. In that case, normally that type of chairperson would not vote, in order to prevent uninformed influence of the team's decision results. However, if the chair is an active member of the system with program responsibilities, such as managing one or more programs, then it might be appropriate for that person to participate in the voting by the team. Frequently, the chair of budget teams is the chief academic officer of the system, which is often recommended as well.

An effectual chair is one who facilitates team activities impartially without advocacy or expressions of support or opposition to any program package before the group. If the chair makes affirmative or negative comments about programs before the team, it may have an undue influence upon team members or even foster a chilling effect on member contributions to the discussions.

Characteristics of an effective chairperson (Exhibit 8.1) were developed by the South Africa Scouting Association for use by parent committees, and several of the points included in that list are worth consideration by budget advisory team chairpersons (South Africa Scouts, 2009):

Exhibit 8.1   Characteristics of an Effective Chairperson

Characteristic	Rationale
Friendly and approachable	Establishes friendly and cooperative atmosphere
Calm and even temperament	Creates stability and reduces volatility
Full disclosure of information	Supports clear thinking and open minds
Follows parliamentary procedure	Fosters efficiency and sound decision making

Once the chair calls the budget advisory team to order for the purpose of learning about and evaluating budget package proposals, it is incumbent upon the program managers to provide the appropriate information about their program and program packages.

Program Manager Responsibilities and Roles

Program managers, usually one per program, have a number of responsibilities to the team. Of course, program managers may be a member of the team, but they also are responsible for communicating about their program packages to the full membership of the team. The role of the program manager is to do the following:

- Deliver a presentation to the budget advisory team to give an overview of the program and a description of each package.
  - Demonstrate connections to the system's mission and goals if possible.
  - Highlight creativity in the program package configurations.
  - Refrain from presenting win/lose or either/or propositions if possible.
  - Facilitate discussion of personnel by position as a group, not individually.

- Packages may be altered or modified, but the cost parameters remain the same or less after modification.
  - Staffing pattern changes must clearly illustrate which duties will change and who will do what after the modification.
  - Staffing patterns need to be practical, feasible, and realistic.
- Presentations must be delivered within the established time limit (usually ten to fifteen minutes per program).
  - Time limits will be enforced, but one-minute warnings will be given.
- Presentations will be in the order used in the budget advisory team resource manual (in order by code or alphabetically).
- Presentations will follow team rules about electronic media and handouts.
  - Electronic media must be standardized for all program manager presenters in order to prevent undue influence.
  - Handout material is usually prohibited because of the need for fairness across presenters. The information in program packages should be written and described sufficiently for team member understanding.
- Answer questions from the members of the team during the designated period—usually after all presentations have been made.
  - No interruptions are permitted during program manager presentations.

Program managers need to be mindful of these procedures and follow them appropriately.

Budget Team Member Roles and Responsibilities

During work sessions of the budget advisory team, members of the group need to be attentive and respectful to presenters. During presentations, some guidelines for team members to consider are stipulated as follows.

- Connect presented information about program packages to the system's mission and goals, if possible, for validity.

- Listen attentively and take notes of key information points.
  - Interruptions of presenters are discouraged during presentations.
  - Show respect to one another, and hear and understand all viewpoints.
- Questions need to be noted, and expressed only during the designated question and answer period.
  - Questions are for obtaining clarification about program packages only.
  - No advocacy or opposition statements are permitted during team meetings.
  - Address issues, not people, and ask questions in a positive way.
- Team members will rank order all budget packages in accordance with instructions.
  - A Q-sort (value judgment) nominal group process will be utilized to obtain rankings.
  - All ranking activities are completed by team members anonymously, with confidentiality of individual rankings.
- In the event of disputes or ambiguities, the team chair will have final authority for resolution.
- Group consensus will be the decision-making model for ranking, and a parliamentary vote will be used to determine closure of the budget advisory team's work.

These ground rules are for members of the budget advisory team, who may choose to modify, add to, or delete any of the rules.

Visitor and Observer Roles and Responsibilities

It is frequently pointed out that school systems are public bodies, and as a rule, deliberations of public bodies are required or advised to be conducted in public settings. Generally, advisory groups are not considered governing bodies since they do not possess decision-making power. Some states exclude advisory committees from open meeting laws, but others expressly apply open meeting laws to advisory committees (Schwing, 2006–2008).

Budget advisory teams are groups that have purely fact-finding, informational, recommendatory, or advisory purposes with no decision-making power. However, as stated in an Oklahoma law case, "If an informed citizenry is to meaningfully participate in government or at least understand why government acts affecting their daily lives are taken, the process of decision making as well as the end results must be conducted in full view of the governed" (*Oklahoma Association of Municipal Attorneys v. State*, 1978, pp. 1313–1314). Consequently, it is advisable and beneficial for visitors and observers to watch budget team proceedings.

This suggestion does not extend to permitting visitors or observers to participate in budget advisory team discussions or deliberations. The team needs to be free of unwarranted pressure or influence from individuals or groups who may wish to oppose or support a particular program or budget package proposal. For that reason, the following ground rules are important for visitors and observers.

- Visitors and observers are welcome to watch budget advisory team proceedings from seating designated by the chairperson outside the area occupied by the team.
- Visitors may attend only as observers, and comments to the team will not be permitted during its deliberations.
- Members of the team who have questions for observers or visitors may direct them to an individual in private but not during team proceedings.

Naturally, the budget advisory team may establish its own rules relative to participation by nonmembers of the group, but experience has demonstrated that when budget deliberations are influenced by biased individuals or groups, the final result is highly susceptible to bias and conflict.

OVERVIEW OF THE PRIORITY-SETTING PROCESS

After the program packages have been prepared, the budget advisory team has convened and begun its work, and program managers have presented their packages to the team, the program packages will be ranked by the team. Packages are ranked by the team in order of priority—that is, which of all the packages is absolutely the most necessary for funding, which package is next, and so on. It's important to note that individual packages are ranked independently of their program, and a program's packages are not ranked together as a group.

For example, in Exhibit 8.2, consider the following excerpt of package ranking conducted by a Minnesota school district. Note the order in which program packages were selected for funding.

Also in Exhibit 8.2, note the order of priority given packages by the budget advisory team. For example, the media and technology base package was rated number 1, before all other packages. However, its next package (base +1%) wasn't funded until number 21. Also, note that the music and fine arts base package was funded at number 7, but the next level (base +1%) doesn't appear in the top 24 packages. Also, note that the elementary instruction current package (100%) was ranked number 11, but its two earlier packages were ranked at numbers 3 and 8.

The point of this illustration is that packages are ranked independently of the other packages in the same program. Any package at any level may be ranked higher than any package of another program. Also, a lower-increment-level package will always be ranked before a higher-increment-level package of the same program, since it represents a lower level of service. The process of ranking for any and all programs starts with the basic packages and then to subsequent higher-level packages, but not necessarily consecutively.

Exhibit 8.2, the system team determined for valid reasons that the media and technology current level package (100%) was to be ranked before the junior high instruction current level package. So, hypothetically, if the system were to have only $100,444,072 available, the media and technology package would be funded but the junior high instruction current package would not. Any program's packages could even be ranked higher than the base package (minimum) of another program.

Exhibit 8.2 Excerpt of Package Ranking Order (24 out of 110) for a Minnesota School System, 2001

Rank Order	Program/Package Description	Package Cost	Cumulative Cost
1	Media/Technology - Base Component	$1,366,244	$1,366,244
2	Guidance/Health - Base Component	$2,676,843	$4,043,087
3	Elementary Instruction - Base Component	$32,035,670	$36,078,757
4	Senior High Instruction - Base Component	$14,770,359	$50,849,116
5	Custodial/Maintenance - Base Component	$7,003,545	$57,852,661
6	Junior High Instruction - Base Component	$13,903,230	$71,755,891
7	Music and Fine Arts - Base Component	$3,115,830	$74,871,721
8	Elementary Instruction - Base +1% Component	$326,916	$75,198,637
9	Senior High Instruction - Base +1% Component	$150,718	$75,349,355
10	Junior High Instruction - Base +1% Component	$141,832	$75,491,187
11	Elementary Instruction - Current Component	$326,870	$75,818,057
12	Human Resources - Base Component	$536,403	$76,354,460
13	ESL - Base Component	$653,809	$77,008,269
14	Special Education - Base Component	$9,461,913	$86,470,182
15	Transportation - Base Component	$7,291,984	$93,762,166
16	Vocational - Base Component	$1,684,529	$95,446,695
17	Board & Superintendent - Base Component	$640,374	$96,087,069
18	Talented & Gifted - Base Component	$687,877	$96,774,946
19	Business Services - Base Component	$1,955,429	$98,730,375
20	Athletics and Activities - Base Component	$1,699,756	$100,430,131
21	Media/Technology - Base +1% Component	$13,941	$100,444,072
22	Junior High Instruction - Current Component	$141,832	$100,585,904
23	Custodial/Maintenance - Base +1% Component	$71,465	$100,657,369
24	Senior High Instruction - Current Component	$150,718	$100,808,087

It's important to remember that the base package for any given program contains the largest percentage of the total funding for a program, and each increment or package added on after that is a very small percentage of the total for the program.

Ultimately, the budget advisory team determines the final ranking of all packages and submits their ranking recommendation to the superintendent or CEO for review and consideration before submitting it to the governing body. The superintendent has discretion to modify or change component rankings before presenting it to the governing body for review and adoption. Of course, the same discretion for modifying the team's recommendation rests with the governing board.

Ordinarily, it is somewhat unusual for administrators or governing bodies to change budget advisory teams' rankings. The nature of the in-depth preparation and study process conducted by the budget team represents one of the highest and best processes for decision making. Second-guessing of collaborative team decision making isn't liable to produce healthy relationships within the system.

Criteria for Determining Rank Order of Packages

Occasionally, school systems develop some specific criteria for considering funding priorities for packages. Suggested criteria for judging how to rank packages and determining net value of proposed budget packages with others may include the following for individual packages:

1. Extent of critical relationship to the mission of the district, and the level of congruity with the system's goals and objectives for improvement

2. The degree that the package provides for minimum health, safety, legal, and educational support requirements

3. Extent of necessity to meet educational levels prescribed by state standards and other accrediting organizations, and inclusion of services necessary for efficient and effective operations

4. Provision of some enhancements or increased efficiency or effectiveness of educational, instructional, and support services

5. The degree that the package provides for student differences, interests, and abilities, and provides resources to improve the quality of teaching, support services, capital equipment and facilities

6. Demonstration of desirability, but not necessity, for the efficient and effective operation of the system

Needless to say, the system may choose to determine its own scoring rubric for ranking budget packages, but the six criteria here are provided for illustration purposes.

Budget Advisory Team Activities in Priority Setting

Once the advisory team has the materials and data for ranking program packages, the following steps may then be implemented.

1. A budget priority-setting meeting is convened. All members of the budget advisory team (which includes all program managers) must attend and participate. Normally, nonattendance generates forfeiture of voting rights in the ranking process.

2. Procedures for the budget priority-setting meeting are as follows:

   a. Introductions and review of ground rules are provided (no evaluative comments, questions for information only, time limits must be honored, etc.).

   b. Notebooks containing package descriptions (provided by the business office) are distributed, if not done beforehand.

   c. Program manager presentations will be given, with an explanation of the program area, the packages, and the gains/losses incumbent in each package.

      i. Presentations may not exceed a given number of minutes per program, usually ten to fifteen minutes each.

      ii. Audiovisual presentations are required to be within types agreed upon by the budget advisory team.

   d. Questions of program managers will be permitted at the conclusion of all presentations *for information or clarification only.* No comments may be made about efficacy or necessity of any program components.

3. Preliminary ranking will be conducted using a Q-sort (weighted voting) technique (see next section), and all rankings will be *anonymous* by each member of the team.

4. Ranking must not reorder packages *within* a program area. A program's base (initial) package must receive the highest ranking of any package within that program area. Successive packages may receive equal or lesser point value, but never a higher value than a preceding package within that program area.

5. Ranking will be done across all packages, using a maximum four-point scale.

6. After the committee has ranked the packages, point assignments are tallied and used to rank the packages in priority order. At this time, the team will review the rankings and permit additional presentation time, usually two- to three-minute statements by each program manager. After comments are heard, team members will then again rank order the packages using a second round of Q-sort procedures.

7. The second listing will be published, and the team will then review the final list. Motions, debate, and parliamentary procedure will then be used to make any changes in rank order. Votes may be by written or electronic ballot, always anonymously.

8. Once the budget advisory team agrees that the rankings are completed, no more ranking is needed. Closure of deliberations is normally agreed upon by the team with a parliamentary procedural vote. Anonymity of voting is recommended.

9. The final ranking will then be tabulated, published, and submitted to the superintendent for review and recommendation to the governing board for review and approval.

Board Action Following Advisory Team Recommendations

It is recommended that the governing board receive a report of the budget advisory team rankings followed by a very brief (three to five minutes each) presentation from each program manager, presenting information about the program packages and the nature of the package provisions. The board normally follows the same steps as the budget advisory team in obtaining an understanding of each program package. This type of activity is best accomplished in a special study session, which should be held for obtaining information for the governing board. Lobbying or special interest group demands are not recommended at this point in the process and are better deferred to a regular meeting of the board, in which board action may be effectuated.

Once the board has established a preliminary ranking of the packages, final determinations of ranking may be done in a regular public meeting with formal voting and parliamentary procedures. During this session, the board may accept public comments from constituents in accordance with normal procedures.

Public presentations on the budget may also be scheduled to inform the community of the budget action taken and the priorities within the budget that have been established by the budget advisory team, the superintendent, and the governing board. The governing board reviews all of the budget package rankings, considers other information received from the organization and community, and proceeds to accept or modify package rankings as deemed appropriate in their collective judgment.

After due consideration, the governing board accepts and approves a budget package ranking, and the budget is approved and established. Once revenues are known, the packages are funded in the order of ranking or precedence and in alignment with revenues available. Obviously, as more funds become available, more packages are funded. If there are insufficient revenues to fund all packages, the unfunded packages become abandoned.

PRESENTING BUDGET PACKAGES

General Budget Package Presentation Suggestions

There are some key points to be clarified with respect to how budget packages need to be presented to the budget advisory team, the governing board, and to the general public (if a public school system). These points include the following:

- It is a good idea to avoid focus on the protection of line items: staffing, supplies, travel, maintenance, and so on. It is more critical to focus on changes in *how* the program or service is delivered and at what level of quality.
- Acknowledge that investment in personnel services has significant impact in terms of percentage of overall total costs, and changes in personnel should be described in terms of effect on programs. However, positions may be identified by job title (i.e., teachers, secretarial-clerical, etc.).

- Uniform assumptions (data from the system financial database) need to be used in package construction, such as
  - Enrollment increases or decreases must be agreed upon and used by all program managers.
  - Current levels of funding need to be described in terms of impact on service or program delivery.
  - Staffing effects need to be communicated in terms of full-time equivalents (FTE) or portions—individual names must never be used:
    - Professional and support staff positions at different funding levels need to be described clearly.
    - Differential delivery of services and programs for reasons of equity or identified need require careful explanation of how the differences were determined.
- Presenters may use other personnel in clarifying how their programs/services are configured.
- Program managers may describe how they utilized planning committees of teachers, parents, students, and administrators (representatives).
- Helpful information includes how program service affects numbers of students.
- "Givens" must be clarified. For example, one school system had a critical need for updating technology. The governing board stipulated that a large sum of money for new technology improvements was to be set aside and exempted from the rankings. In effect, the ranking of the set-aside technology improvements was above number 1 on the priority list.
- "Benchmarking" information about comparisons to other districts is often useful; however, care is required because comparisons (i.e., transportation costs) may vary by conditions.
- Each program manager must be prepared to be queried about specifics (for clarification, not advocacy)—for example, an explanation of how an individual package was developed may be requested.

Effective Strategies for Package Presentations

Many presentations use connectivity, transparency, and other conditions in explaining how a package proposal might look or work. Some sample characteristics have been derived from several well-planned presentations:

- *Connectivity.* For example: "The district strategic plan calls for learning technology expansion, and this proposal provides resources for use in addressing that objective."
- *Impact on students.* For example: "With this proposal, tennis and volleyball would become ninth- through twelfth-grade sports only, and approximately sixty student athletes would not have a program."
- *Health and safety.* For example: "One enhancement we are requesting is for the addition of paraprofessional help for supervision of playground activities, which would greatly improve our safety and security."

- *Transparency.* For example: "The financial services program provides support to all programs in the district—it contains ten employees. Support is provided for payroll for 2,000 people, $85 million in expenditures are accounted for and bills are paid, financial accounting is provided, as well as direct support to food service, transportation, and employee insurance programs. With the reduction package, staff development, school elections, and employee benefits options would be reduced and services would be terminated."
- *Impact on staff.* For example: "If this component is not funded, we will be paying employees once a month instead of twice a month." (Reduction of the cost of payroll generation.)
- *Impact on facilities and staff.* For example: "At the 95% level, cleaning services would be reduced. Cleaning every day would not be possible, since eleven custodial positions are eliminated, with 24,000 square feet/each, resulting in 264,000 square feet left without daily services. Some rooms will only be cleaned four times a week."
- *Humor.* For example: "My program increments are named 'drowned'—90%, 'sinking'—95%, 'treading'—100%, 'bronze'—103%, and 'silver'—106%."

How *Not* to Present a Budget Package

There are some types of presentation strategies that are less than effective and that may have a tendency to produce a reverse effect, in which support for the package is diminished.

- *Evasion and equivocation.* For example: "If we have to cut, the cuts will come out of people, and that means that the elementary principals will have to decide who will be let go." (Note: This approach does not speak to what those positions do—better to address what activities, services, programs, or goals might be terminated or abandoned.)
- *Scornful supplication.* For example: "I can't stand up here and share with you in fifteen minutes what I have given my entire life to build in my program." (Note: This strategy appeals to emotion and does not address the value of the activity.)
- *Obfuscation and concealment.* For example: "Please don't share what I'm going to propose to you, because I haven't discussed any of the possible changes with any of the coaches. Some of these proposals would make some of the coaches upset." (Note: This approach asks that the budget committee conspire to change the nature of a program without revealing any information to the people affected by such changes—this is incongruent with participatory decision making and organizational integrity.)
- *Exhortation and threat.* For example: "You need to know that if this isn't funded, then parents and community people are going to be very upset and you'll be to blame." (Note: Hints at intimidation that the team may be facing dire consequences. It also threatens a vague penalty if the presenter's program isn't funded, and it is not considered to be offered in a spirit of cooperative collaboration.)

Clearly, program managers and program package presenters are well advised to carefully consider using rational and valid consequences to budget allocation modification, rather than emotional or political approaches, in order to garner accurate and reasonable responses to their program components.

REACHING CONSENSUS WITH Q-SORT METHODOLOGY

In research and statistical analysis, there are a number of nominal group techniques that facilitate reaching consensus on various variables with large groups of people. In performance-based budgeting, the preferred approach for achieving consensus is by ranking program packages in order of priority.

The Q-methodology approach was developed decades ago, but McKeown and Thomas adapted it for use in the social sciences (McKeown & Thomas, 1988). The process is user-friendly and was adapted for use in performance-based budgeting because it produces a very clear and reasonable list of ranked variables in the order of priority set by the group—in this case, the budget advisory team or the governing board.

How to Rank Budget Packages in Priority Order

In the Q- (Quintile) sort technique, group consensus requires each member of the ranking group to assign a value to each of the budget packages (separately and independently from their program) under consideration. The value may be any of five levels, ranging from zero to four (0 to 4) points. The total number of points that a member of the group may assign is restricted so that all variables may not be rated at the highest value level. The values for all packages assigned by all members of the group are then averaged, and the average value is used to sort the variables by their accumulated totals.

Each component (or increment) of a given program is to be considered as a stand-alone, independent budget proposal. Ratings will be completed by each member of the budget advisory team or committee (program managers, administrators, teacher-staff members, parent-community members, students, etc.). All members of the budget advisory team have equal status in determining the rank order of program components or increments. The final product of the team will comprise a recommendation to the superintendent and the governing board.

Criteria for Consideration in Assigning Values

The following criteria are recommended for consideration in ascribing a value to each component (package):

- Alignment of the proposed program component with the system mission (how this program conforms to or facilitates the mission of the system)
- Criticality of the proposed program component in accomplishing the mission (how important this program is in terms of the system's aims and purposes)

- Demonstrated connections between the proposed program component and effective performance or productivity (how this program component improves the quality of the organization and how that is evidenced)
- Cost-benefit relationships of the proposed program component (what value the organization gets for the cost, and their determination of its worth)

Overview of Determining Package Values and Collective Ranking Procedures

Each program package or component is to be assigned a number of points (five levels or quintiles), from none (0) to a maximum of four (4), depending upon the value determinations of the rater. Each program component can be rated as follows:

4 points	Highest priority
3 points	High priority
2 points	Moderate priority
1 point	Low priority
0 points	Lowest priority

During the developmental process, program managers will have already ranked their program packages in the order of priority needed for the program to function effectively at any level of funding. It's critical that the manager's package rankings within the program are honored and not undermined.

It's important to understand that for that reason, no program component within a program may be rated higher or lower by the budget advisory team than the original rankings *within the same program* which were ordered in importance by the manager of the program. In other words, an enhancement package of a program may not be rated higher in priority than that same program's recovery or base packages. Responsibility for internal ranking of program components rests only with program managers. In other words, the packages ranked within programs, once set by the program managers, must be honored as the program components are ranked in the priority-setting process.

As mentioned earlier, each budget advisory team member will be given a maximum number of points that may be assigned to all program components. The number of points is twice the number of packages to be ranked. So if there were fifty program packages to be ranked, the number of points would be twice the number of packages, or in this case 100. If the number of packages is 100, each member of the team would have 200 points to assign.

Please note: Ratings by individual members that exceed the maximum number of points normally are disqualified and may not be included in the consensus rankings.

This procedure, in effect, allows individual group members to assign values in a variety of ways. For example if there are fifty program packages and 100 points to assign, an individual might assign 2 points to all fifty program packages. They might also award 4 points to twenty-five (or half) of the program packages. The experience of systems that have used the technique has been that abuses are extremely rare and that budget advisory team members are highly conscientious about honoring the rectitude of the procedure.

An example of a Q-sort product is shown in the following Exhibit 8.3.

Exhibit 8.3 Example of a Budget Team's Q-Sort Values for Program Packages

Rank	Package Name	Pkg Cost	Point Total	Point Mean	Cumulative Total	A	B	C	D	E	F	G	H	I
										Team Members' Ratings				
1	Elem Instr 95%	$5,051,986	31	3.44	$5,051,986	4	2	3	4	5	4	4	2	3
2	MidSchInstr 95%	$2,743,825	29	3.22	$7,795,811	4	2	2	3	3	4	5	3	3
3	Technology 95%	$389,282	28	3.50	$8,185,093	4	2	4	2	4	4		4	4
4	SpecEd 95%	$4,436,134	26	2.89	$12,621,227	1	2	2	5	3	3	2	3	5
5	Transp 95%	$1,343,443	25	2.78	$13,964,670	1	2	3	3	3	4	1	3	5
6	HS Inst 95%	$3,108,163	24	2.67	$17,072,833	4	2	2	2	3	4	4	1	2
7	Activ 95%	$657,431	23	2.56	$17,730,264	4	2	2	2	3	2	5	1	2
8	K12 Inst 95%	$1,564,321	23	2.56	$19,294,585	4	2	3	1	3	3	3	2	2
9	Facil 95%	$3,200,911	23	2.56	$22,495,496	2	2	3	2	5	4	1	2	2
10	Tech I 95%	$1,252,683	22	2.44	$23,748,179	2	2	3	2	5	3	1	2	2
11	Admin Cntrl 95%	$1,682,842	20	2.22	$25,431,021	4	2	2	1	2	4	1	2	2
12	Curr 95%	$323,375	20	2.22	$25,754,396	1	2	2	4	3	3	1	2	2
13	ElemInstr 100%	$265,914	19	2.38	$26,020,310	3	2	1	2	4		3	2	2
14	Media 95%	$789,688	18	2.00	$26,809,998	2	2	2	3	1	1	3	2	3
15	MidSchInstr 100%	$144,412	17	2.13	$26,954,410	4	2	2	2	1	1	4	1	1
16	Health 95%	$323,799	16	1.78	$27,278,209	1	2	2	2	2	3	1	1	2
17	Counseling 95%	$796,341	16	1.78	$28,074,550	1	2	2	2	3	2	1	1	2
18	Admin Bldg 95%	$1,848,942	15	1.67	$29,923,492	1	2	2	1	1	3	1	2	2
19	HS Inst 100%	$163,588	13	1.63	$30,087,080	4	1	1	1		1	3	1	1
20	Suppl 95%	$2,106,374	13	2.17	$32,193,454		2	2	2	3	3	1	1	
	(20 pkgs out of 54)	Total			$32,193,454	51	39	45	46	57	56	45	35	47

125

In the Exhibit 8.3, a sample of member rankings (nine in number) of individual program packages (20 out of 54 packages) is presented. The rankings show how this small sample of individuals ranked individual packages and how the composite rankings were then determined. The data are extrapolated from an actual school system's process, and the data illustrate how a resultant package priority list with funding is built collaboratively with little enmity.

As illustrated, it's important to note that *some* programs' packages (i.e., elementary instruction 100%—current level) may be ranked higher than lower packages from *other* programs (i.e., media, health, and counseling—all at the 95% recovery level). Interpreting these data indicate that the collective wisdom of the group felt that the 100% elementary program package needed to be a higher priority than the other programs' 95% packages. This is not an uncommon occurrence in the process.

Flexibility of Priority Funding

Interestingly, the prioritization or ranking of program packages isn't dependent upon knowledge of the level of funding or revenue that will be available to the system. By ranking program packages and their incumbent costs, a priority list of packages is developed, which may be funded once revenues are sufficient to allow the allocation for including a program package in the final budget. Paradoxically, school systems with diminishing revenues as well as school systems with increasing revenues find the package prioritization process useful, since in many states and provinces the exact amount of financial support provided, or permitted under legislation, by state or provincial governments may not be known until rather late in the budgeting process. The adaptability of the performance-based budget to fluctuating revenues is in fact one of its strengths. Once the level of funding is known, a line is drawn on the ranked list at that point; the packages above the line are funded, and those below the line are not (Poston, Stone, & Muther, 1992).

SUMMARY

This chapter provides the foundational information for the budget advisory team's proceedings, organization, and work. Using the procedures discussed, the team receives presentations that explain program packages from program managers; evaluates the information supplied against system mission, goals, and objectives; and collectively determines the rank order for funding program packages. In the next chapter, specific courses of action are provided for developing a recommendation to the governing board with program package priorities, and for further fine-tuning by the board—leading to adoption of a budget that has built-in adaptability in accord with funding available.

9

Building the Budget Recommendation

One of the key functions of the governing board is to approve the final budget for the system. It needs to be a tool to achieve the goals and objectives of the system in an equitable manner. The meaning of equity was defined by President Reagan's Commission on Excellence in Education (1983) nearly three decades ago:

> All, regardless of race or economic status, are entitled to a fair chance and to the tools for developing their individual powers of mind and spirit to the utmost.

Universal commitment to the educational needs of all students encourages systems to get over the propensity to fund by formula or "head count." One of the major accomplishments of governing boards is to enact policies and goals to level the playing field across schools. Examples of the challenge abound. One of the most striking differences noted in many school systems is the disparity in teacher experience between schools in depressed economic areas, which have less experienced or novice teachers, and schools in wealthy neighborhoods, which have highly experienced faculty. The "one size fits all" approach ignores one of the fundamental precepts of educational psychology—students have individual differences.

INTRODUCTION

Once the budget advisory team has been assembled, the operational procedures have been determined, and the program managers have prepared program packages for consideration by the team, the team may go on with its core work: the preparation of a recommendation to the governing board. In this chapter, the procedures and deliberations leading to consensus on budget decisions will be explored and presented.

BUDGET ADVISORY TEAM OPERATIONS

Budget advisory teams are created from a diverse cross section of the school system community. Membership includes program managers, central administrators (excluding the superintendent or board members), parents, patrons and business representatives, principals, support staff, and teachers. The protocol for this group's business meetings needs to be determined and established prior to commencement of deliberations and discussions. Some of the aspects of the group protocol are described next.

Team Meeting Arrangements

It is important that all team members have equal votes and equal opportunities for discussion, participation, and presentation of ideas. The best room arrangement for budget team deliberations is one in which the seating arrangement for participants is egalitarian in nature. Round, square, or rectangular seating arrangements are practical, but the configuration needs to provide similar space, visibility, and access for all locations. Every member of the team should be able to easily see and hear any other member of the group.

Meeting Management

As pointed out earlier in this text, the chair of the group is recommended to be the chief academic officer of the school system. To assist the chairperson, a vice-chair needs to be designated for leadership if the chairperson becomes unavailable. The chief financial officer of the system needs to serve as the data manager for the team—keeping track of costs, financial coding, and accounting information.

The chair, or his or her designee, needs to manage the deliberations of the group in accord with normal parliamentary procedure. Some of the elements of parliamentary procedure include the following (Lingle & Feinberg, 2005):

BASIC PRINCIPLES OF PARLIAMENTARY PROCEDURE

1. Parliamentary procedure facilitates the transaction of business and promotes cooperation and harmony.

2. All members have equal rights, privileges, and obligations. The will of the majority must be carried out, and the rights of the minority must be preserved.

3. A quorum must be present for the group to act.

4. Full and free discussion of every motion is a basic right.

5. Only one question at a time can be considered at any given time.

6. The chair should be strictly neutral.

The chair manages business of the team by calling the meeting(s) to order, taking (or delegating) roll call, recognizing individuals who wish to speak, facilitating group action by motions and majority vote, and ruling on questions or issues that come to the group.

In this manner, team business may be conducted with a minimum of confusion and a reasonable degree of decorum and fairness.

Mode of Decision Making

There are many options available to the budget advisory team for making decisions relative to budget matters and program package rank ordering. For example, the team could use the Q-sort methodology, the matched-pairs ranking procedure, parliamentary procedure, or even a "town hall" type of process. Experience has demonstrated that the parliamentary procedure and town hall approach share one key disadvantage—discussions and votes are open and public.

Most systems in performance-based budgeting have opted to use the nominal group technique of the Q methodology to establish the initial rank ordering of packages. However, in the event of close rankings of competing packages, the matched-pairs technique resolves narrow rankings, draws, or ties. This technique is explained later in this chapter.

General decisions of the group are best handled with parliamentary procedure with motions, seconds, and votes. Examples of where this is applicable include motions, votes, adjournment, group rules, and similar matters. Ground rules are described in Chapter 8 and later in this chapter.

Once the ground rules are agreed upon, the team carries out the work of the group, culminating in the budget package ranking process.

Ancillary Procedures for Budget Advisory Teams

At this point in the process, the following tasks need to be accomplished and completed:

1. Packages have been prepared for each program area. Program managers have been assigned to each of the program areas, and the managers have prepared the four to five (or more) packages for their program(s) in accordance with previous directions.

2. All packages for each program must be listed on a form; a copy of a suggested form was provided in Chapter 7 (Exhibit 7.1). This form should be a different color than the other two forms.

3. Each program package must be summarized on *one page*. A suggested form was provided in Chapter 7 (Exhibit 7.2).

4. Each package must have all costs summarized on a second page; a sample of that form was included in Chapter 7 (Exhibit 7.3).

5. All package forms should have been collected, and the forms should have been collated into a notebook containing all program package forms. Each program area must have a section consisting of the package list form first, and then a description form and a cost analysis form for each package. Packages should be in the order of priority established by the manager. It is best if the forms are different colors, for ease of access.

Proposed Ground Rules and Process

A meeting of the budget advisory team should then be convened to complete the budget package priority-setting process. With all members present, suggested procedures for the team meeting are as follows:

1. Introductions and review of ground rules (see Chapter 8):
   a. Evaluative comments are not permitted (any inquiry which implies a degree of advocacy or opposition).
   b. No comments will be made about efficacy or necessity of any program components.
   c. Questions may be asked for information only, not disagreement or challenge.
   d. Time limits must be honored.
   e. Other ground rules as agreed upon.

2. Distribution of notebooks containing package descriptions (provided by the financial office).

3. Presentations by program managers given in the order of budget codification:
   a. Program areas must be described and defined.
   b. The range of packages must be described.
   c. Any gains or losses incumbent in each package are described.
   d. Program manager presentations may not exceed five to seven minutes per program as determined by the chair.
   e. Audiovisual presentations are limited to use of media and techniques authorized by the group.

Preliminary ranking of packages will be conducted using the primary nominal group technique. The team needs to be reminded that ranking must not reorder packages *within* a program area. A program's base (first) package must receive the highest ranking of any package *within* that program area. Successive packages may receive equal or lesser point value, but never a higher value than a preceding package within that program area.

Additional Criteria for Judging the Efficacy of Program Packages

Some teams have agreed-upon uniform criteria for program package ranking, such as evaluating packages with the following parameters:

- The nature and extent of critical relationship to mission, goals, and plans of the system
- The degree to which enhancement or expansion of the mission is fostered, and how minimum health, safety, legal, and educational support requirements are met
- The extent of necessity to meet educational services prescribed by state standards and other accrediting organizations, and the degree of inclusion of services necessary for efficient and effective operations
- Whether or not the provision of some enhancement or increased efficiency or effectiveness for educational, instructional, and support services is supported
- The nature of congruence with student differences, interests, and abilities
- The manner in which programs and services will provide resources to improve the quality of teaching, support services, capital equipment, and educational environments
- The apparent beneficial impact upon the efficient and effective operations of the system

Program Evaluation and Reconsideration

Once the committee has ranked the packages, and point assignments are tallied and used to rank the packages in priority order, the team may, upon agreement, evaluate the preliminary rankings. Additional statements by program managers may be permitted, but they should be limited to only a few minutes (two to three minutes) for reconsideration of a package ranking. After comments are heard, team members may then again rank order the packages using the decision process selected earlier.

The second listing of package ranks needs to be published and disseminated. The committee may then review the final list again. It is possible that the team may choose to use motions, debate, and parliamentary procedure to make any changes in rank order. For anonymity, votes may be written or cast by electronic ballot.

Deciding on the Final Ranking and Configuration

Once accepted by the team by vote, the final ranking needs to be tabulated, published, and submitted to the superintendent for final approval and recommendation to the governing board. Board rankings are suggested to follow the same steps as the budget advisory team at a special study session, but with program manager presentations of shorter duration.

Of course, governing board voting and approval needs to be as prescribed by law. Once the ranks are modified or established, board approval must be carried out by public voting and normal parliamentary procedure.

Matched-Pairs Nominal Group Technique (Optional)

Often, governing boards may wish to "tweak" rankings within a short band of ranked program packages. A suitable approach for ranking a band of packages, fewer than twelve in number, is the matched-pairs ranking process.

Basically, the matched-pairs ranking procedure is an adaptation of the recursive ranking process described in the *Mathematics of Voting* (Center for Teaching and Learning, 2010). In the recursive ranking process, a selection of no more than twelve packages is ranked by voting by a group. The item that is the winner of first place overall is declared the winner, is listed as number 1, and is eliminated from the list. The voting is conducted a second time, and the winner is placed in second place on the list. The voting is conducted repeatedly until all members of the band of items are eliminated as winner and placed on the list following the earlier winners. At that point, all packages are ranked.

This information is then used by the governing board to rerank the band of items in question. The procedure is illustrated in Exhibit 9.1.

Once the governing board has agreed on and approved a configuration of package ranks for budget allocations, the ranked packages will then be funded in order of precedence in accordance with revenues available.

COMMONLY ASKED QUESTIONS ABOUT PERFORMANCE-BASED BUDGETING

Questions frequently asked about the performance-based-budgeting process with responses are provided in the following sections. Responses have been obtained from school systems that have implemented the process.

1. Will what we do make a difference?

Absolutely! Each program area will develop at least three package proposals which reflect the priorities for that area. However, this does not mean that everything or anything will be funded. The initial choice to be made is if a program gets 0% or 96%. Therefore, the 96% package is very important for placing a program in the budget. Obviously, many areas will not receive their 100% or enhancement (100 + %) packages since the total expenditures of the district will need to decrease due to diminishing revenues.

The packages from all program areas will be ranked in priority order by the budget advisory team, which is made up of program managers, parents, principals, teachers, classified staff, business representatives, and students. The program managers will need to articulate the program packages and priorities

Exhibit 9.1 Matched-Pairs Ranking Procedure

Directions:

1. Use clear-out voting or consolidation to reduce the list of items (program packages or increments) to twelve or fewer in number.
2. Write the twelve (12) items on the form below, in the numbered blanks.
3. Work your way through the chart, circling the number of the item you prefer in each paired choice. All items will be paired with all other items, and you will "vote" for the one you feel that is the more important one of the pair. For example, in the top box, you will vote for item 1 or 2, 1 or 3, 1 or 4, etc.
4. When finished choosing, enter the number of times you voted for each item in Column A. Then in Column B, rank the items by the number of votes: i.e., 1 for the item you voted for most, and 12 for the item you voted for least.
5. When all team members are finished, groups will add their tallies to get a group total from Column A. Record the group tally in Column C.
6. In Column D, record the rank order of the items with 1 being the one with the most "votes" and 12 the least. The final ranking will be the priority order agreed upon by the total group.

1 2										
1 3	2 3									
1 4	2 4	3 4								
1 5	2 5	3 5	4 5							
1 6	2 6	3 6	4 6	5 6						
1 7	2 7	3 7	4 7	5 7	6 7					
1 8	2 8	3 8	4 8	5 8	6 8	7 8				
1 9	2 9	3 9	4 9	5 9	6 9	7 9	8 9			
1 10	2 10	3 10	4 10	5 10	6 10	7 10	8 10	9 10		
1 11	2 11	3 11	4 11	5 11	6 11	7 11	8 11	9 11	10 11	
1 12	2 12	3 12	4 12	5 12	6 12	7 12	8 12	9 12	10 12	11 12

Exhibit 9.1 (Continued)

Program Package	A Your Totals	B Your Ranking	C Group Totals	D Group Ranking
1				
2				
3				
4				
5				
6				
7				
8				
9				
10				
11				
12				

during discussion as well as have a global perspective of the district priorities. The meetings of the budget advisory team will be open to the public to observe, but not to participate. The public will have the opportunity to react to the recommended prioritized packages during a public hearing, when scheduled by the governing board as it considers the budget team's recommendation.

2. What about requests from staff?

Staff will be given ample opportunity to provide input to each program area during the development of program packages. Program managers will take steps to elicit suggestions from staff during their program planning.

3. What about salary and benefit increases?

The process intentionally deals with a temporary "placeholder" for all staff salaries, which is an average salary for each type of position for the prior year. This prevents inconsistency and simplifies the work of program managers.

Salary determinations and/or negotiations proceed normally to define salaries and benefits for various positions. Once a budget is adopted, the financial services division will replace and reconcile new salaries with the budgeted positions' temporary placeholder salary amount. As should be expected, salary allocations may affect the final funds available for package allocations and the rank-order funding line.

4. Do packages need to be typed on the forms contained in the program managers' manual?

All program managers may request electronic files containing the required forms in word processing format. The packages may be typed, saved, and submitted electronically. Otherwise, the packages may be typed or written on the sample forms and submitted on paper. It is advisable for program managers to keep copies of all submissions in a safe place.

5. Do the package proposals have to match exactly the designated percentage levels (i.e., 96%)?

No. Additionally, no package proposal may exceed the designated cost level, but package proposals may be less than the designated cost level. For example, a base proposal, such as 92%, could be any level less than that. The percentage level designated is considered the maximum cost level for that package proposal.

6. Who will be the representatives on the budget advisory team?

The first priority for representatives is to select individuals who represent all major operations of the system—teachers, support staff, parents, patrons, administrative heads, and program managers. Emphasis also needs to be on the selection of individuals who are committed to attending all sessions. Students, business representatives, and others may also be considered.

7. What should the presentations to the district advisory team include?

The presentations are intended to highlight the information provided in program package descriptions. Program managers should not be distributing new information or handouts in a presentation. Presentations will be given a time limit and should not be an elaborate production or performance—just the facts.

8. When are the advisory team meetings?

Budget advisory team members will be given a schedule of meetings, probably within a two-week time frame. It is anticipated that meetings will be three to four hours in duration, and four meetings will be scheduled initially, with more meetings later if required. Saturdays may also be considered for meetings to permit informal sessions and a relaxed atmosphere.

9. Who may attend the advisory team meetings?

While all meetings are open to the public for observation, the only people authorized to participate in the discussions and priority determinations will be the advisory team members. Board members, community members, employees, parents, and students are welcome to attend and observe the proceedings, but they may not participate. Of course, any members of the advisory team may consult with anyone deemed appropriate at their discretion outside of regular team meetings.

10. Who will see the packages generated by each program?

Once all the program packages are submitted and ranked by the advisory team and reviewed by the superintendent, they will be presented to the board and printed for publication. The budget packages and approved budget will be considered public documents, available upon request to any individual.

11. How are miscellaneous costs best handled, such as utilities, postage, fixed costs?

All operational costs for programs need to be included in the package costs on a pro rata basis. However, each package needs to be able to function at the base level (first package) so any operational costs for the entire program may have to be included there. Utilities are a distinctly identifiable cost item and may be included in a system support program package for all programs. Allocating utilities across packages is probably not advisable because of the complexities of assuring utilities services to the system. The advisory team may have to discuss similar questions to resolve how some budget components are best handled.

12. How can equity be assured to individual schools within the instructional program packages?

School needs are different, students are different, and facilities are different as well. Program managers need to adjust allocations to school buildings in accordance with the differential needs of the individual schools. Some form of weighted allocation considerations is needed to prevent "one size fits all" in allocations for instruction and instructional support (see Chapter 7).

13. How are the evaluation components of packages to be constructed?

Each package needs to have objectives that the program package will address, and those objectives need to be measurable and to be evaluated for results. All program managers, in consultation with system evaluation and assessment personnel, are responsible for selecting, describing, and using appropriate evaluation procedures for their individual packages. Tangible results and consequences of funding are needed to conduct cost-benefit analysis and to provide feedback for program improvement.

14. Is there evidence to support change in the budgeting process at this time? Why change?

It has been becoming increasingly evident that changes are needed in educational systems to achieve excellence in curriculum and instruction, to secure equal student success in learning, and to assure economic viability within a rapidly changing world. Moreover, resources and revenues to maintain quality within the system have become progressively more difficult to obtain and use. The performance-based budgeting process will enable the system to identify essential goals and objectives for its programs, develop meaningful and research-based operations and services, and give the community tangible connections between system activities, program results, and reasonable costs.

SUMMARY

In this chapter, the strategies for ranking program packages by the budget advisory team are described. The primary approach to rank ordering budget packages is recommended to be the Q methodology described in Chapter 8 (McKeown & Thomas, 1988). Both the budget advisory team and the governing board rank order the budget packages; in the case of two or more packages being ranked at the same priority, a second nominal group strategy is recommended. Participants in the process usually have a number of questions about the process, and responses have been anticipated and provided. Once the deliberations have concluded, and once the governing board has approved the budget configuration, the next and final step is for the system to "close the loop" and evaluate the process and outcome in accordance with the procedure described in the next chapter.

10

Budget Issues and Evaluation

"Accurate and reliable data about educational programs—their results and their costs—are crucial to making informed decisions that will improve the effectiveness of public schools and their investment in America's future" (Robinson, 1987). Extending evaluation to the process of performance-based budgeting also helps assure the school system that its efforts are worth doing. In the Garden City school district (Kansas), the system gave an evaluation form to the members of its budget planning team asking if it was "important to continue the (new) budgeting process." The respondents, twenty in number, voted anonymously with 90% (18) voting yes and 10% (2) voting no. That confirmed for Garden City schools that their budgeting process was valuable and worthwhile.

INTRODUCTION

W. Edwards Deming, the founder of the quality improvement movement, described a critical process by which organizations can evaluate their work and progress and initiate efforts to improve the system (Deming, 1986). His description of the process was simple in its design, but profound in its effect. In this model, quality control and improvement depend upon four elements—goals and direction, organizational action, measurement of results, and examination of findings for further improvement. His model is shown in Exhibit 10.1.

Exhibit 10.1   Quality Improvement Relationships Model

The relationships depicted in the exhibit above are cyclical and continuous. The organization establishes what it wishes to accomplish, implements organizational action, and assesses outcomes to see if the intended goals and objectives are accomplished. In effect, evaluation closes the loop of quality improvement.

This chapter will cite and explore selected budgeting issues, examine the effects of performance-based budgeting, and illustrate an effective method for evaluating the quality of the budgeting process. In addition, a model for participatory decision making will also be presented for consideration.

EXPECTED EFFECTS OF PERFORMANCE-BASED BUDGETING

The marks of performance-based budgeting are openly evident and have been noted in many school systems that have implemented the process. Some of the highlights of performance-based budgeting and the expected benefits include the following effects.

Public Transparency and Quality Improvement

School systems generally serve a community, and system operations need to be open to observation and scrutiny in order to build confidence within the community for establishing quality educational services.

Public school systems often may have a fragile relationship with their communities. Occasionally, two contradictory interests collide and provide a difficult challenge for school leaders. On one hand, communities may desire high levels of quality from their schools; but on the other hand, taxpayers may want high productivity at low levels of cost.

These two factors may not be ignored. One definition of quality is "the degree of excellence at an acceptable price and the control of variability at an acceptable cost" (Broh, 1982). In other words, both the aspiration for quality and the economic demand for financial prudence may need to be addressed in the budgeting process. Without full disclosure and transparency in the process, no budgeting process could routinely be expected to be satisfactory to an interested public constituency.

Moreover, as described in the introduction to this chapter, when the assessed needs of clientele and the organization are considered in light of available resources, quality increments permit the system to flexibly determine the level of quality it can afford. Given the perceptible link of available resources to quality components, it is not unlikely that constituents' values would transform the system's goals toward enhanced levels of quality (Spear, 2009).

Systems are able to utilize the performance-based budgeting process to provide better information about needs of the school system to the community and the costs of differential levels of quality for greater public understanding. It is customarily a useful tool for acquainting the community with not only what the costs are but what quality components the funds deliver.

Allocation Linkage With Measured Results

Organizations need feedback on results and process effectiveness in order to improve over time (Deming, 1986). Schools are no different, and the performance-based budgeting use of evaluation of funding allocations connects feedback on results with program quality, which enables school systems to change, modify, improve, or terminate activities. In effect, school systems are enabled to connect activities of the organization with information about performance and efficacy. In the case of performance-based budgeting, performance (or measured success) drives program component allocations.

Cost-benefit relationships are considered in the performance-based budgeting process; program delivery options and alternatives are developed, located, and evaluated; and priorities are rank ordered for funding within obtainable resources. The performance-based budgeting process focuses on productivity issues—in the vernacular, "How much bang can we get from the buck?" By linking program intentions and purposes (needs, goals, objectives, etc.) with measurement of results, the system is enabled to determine how much value is obtained from various ways and means for programmatic implementation. The better the feedback data, the better the system can make decisions about the viability and suitability of a program component for continuation, modification, or discontinuance.

Commitment and Valuing With Collaborative Teams

Participatory decision making is an important part of the performance-based budgeting process, and the infusion of collaboration produces valuable organizational effects. It is not well known, but teams have been demonstrated to be more effective than individuals in solving problems. This phenomenon displays itself particularly when group tasks require multiple skills, judgments, and experience (Katzenbach & Smith, 1994).

Effective teams are not only committed to their purposes, goals, and processes, but in addition, high-performance teams are committed to each other in supportive ways. Deming alluded to this behavior of groups in his espousal of what he labeled his "theory of psychology." Deming asserted that "in place of competition, we need cooperation" (1993, p. 121). In effect, Deming was calling for win-win management with no losers, in which all participants contribute to the solution of problems. This is reminiscent of the adage, "The whole is greater than the sum of the parts" (attributed to Aristotle).

When groups work together collectively and are focused on team efforts, personal growth and performance are enhanced. Some of the advantages of group team effort include:

- Advantageous use of differential skills in problem solving
- Greater free-flowing information with a flat team structure without hierarchical features
- More cohesively unified and focused vision and direction
- Expanded constructive interactions with team member empowerment
- Enhanced understanding, ownership, and support for team decisions
- Improved quality of decisions

Leadership needs to assume responsibility for development and achievement of the collaborative budget advisory team's functional effectiveness. The nature of the team's organization normally shifts from "top down," fragmented, and competitive characteristics to a team that exemplifies cohesiveness, collaboration, and interactive problem solving.

CLOSING THE LOOP: EVALUATING PERFORMANCE-BASED BUDGETING

There are two points of consideration in evaluating the performance-based budgeting process. First, the impact upon programs and services found within specific program packages warrants evaluation to determine how quality in design and delivery was manifested in the component following implementation, usually on an annualized basis.

Second, evaluation of the process itself is needed in order to determine if the process was effective, how it might be improved, and if it merits continuation as a budgeting tool. Feedback information on the efficacy of program packages enables the improvement of quality over time.

This section will deal with both options for evaluating the performance-based budgeting process and products, and additionally, will address standards guiding program evaluation.

Standards Guiding Program Evaluation

In 1981, a joint committee of organizational representatives conceptualized and developed standards for program evaluation (Joint Committee on Standards for Educational Evaluation, 1994). The standards developed by the committee, which was a consortium of several national professional education organizations, are comprehensive and are organized into four areas with unique guidelines:

1. *Utility standards.* Assure that an evaluation will serve the information needs of intended users.

2. *Feasibility standards.* Stipulate that an evaluation will be realistic, prudent, diplomatic, and frugal.

3. *Propriety standards.* Specify that evaluations will be conducted legally, ethically, and with due regard for the welfare of those involved in the evaluation, as well as those affected by its results.

4. *Accuracy standards.* Seek to assure that an evaluation will reveal and convey technically adequate information about the features that determine worth or merit of the program being evaluated.

The standards are very specific in their delineation of precepts for valid and meaningful program evaluation, and they would be immensely useful to school systems interested in developing and implementing a sound and practical program evaluation process. A summary of the standards and the criteria is provided in Appendix C at the back of the book.

School systems are well advised to consider adoption and use of the program evaluation standards in construction of policy, guidance in program design, and employment in the assessment of program efficacy within performance-based budgeting.

Evaluating Compiled Program Packages

Following the funding allocations to programs, program managers assemble all components into a unified whole and proceed to implement the program. At points along the way of implementation, evaluation needs to be used in a formative fashion. Formative assessment is evaluation within programs while the program is in process.

The concept of formative assessment began in the field of program evaluation. A distinction was suggested between *formative evaluation* and *summative evaluation* when describing two major functions of evaluation (Scriven, 1967). Formative evaluation was intended to foster development and improvement within an ongoing activity (or person, product, program, etc.). On the other hand, summative evaluation was designed to assess whether the results of the program, innovation, person, and so on reflect the original stated goals.

Program Evaluation Criteria

Evaluating a program involves the use of a rubric or set of printed criteria, usually developed prior to program development and always aligned with the program's goals and objectives. In the program package development process, program managers have discretion in designing the evaluation of their program components. However, the system may wish to utilize a generic set of criteria within policy to guide program managers in the development, inclusion, and use of program evaluation. A highly useful body of criteria for program evaluation is used in curriculum management auditing (CMSi, 2009), which may be helpful to school systems. The criteria are as follows:

- Program evaluation procedures are outlined in board policy and/or administrative regulations.
- Procedures for program evaluation include needs assessment, formative evaluation, and periodic summative evaluation.
- Persons conducting the evaluation are both credible and competent, ensuring that findings achieve maximum credibility and acceptance.
- Multiple measures of data collection are used, including quantitative and qualitative measures.
- Reports clearly describe programs, context, purposes, procedures, findings, and recommendations.
- Reports are utilized by key administrators to make timely decisions regarding program effectiveness and continuation.
- Program evaluation designs are practical, cost-effective, and adequately address major political issues.
- Reports identify both strengths and weaknesses of the program and include recommendations to ameliorate weaknesses.
- Data used to evaluate the program are accurate and reliable.
- Procedures used in the evaluation are clearly described.
- All programs are evaluated every three years.
- All proposals for the initiation of new programs include needs assessment data and a description of formative and summative evaluation procedures.

The above criteria provide general guidance to program managers in the development of appropriate evaluation strategies for individual program packages. As the process of performance-based budgeting continues over a period of years, the refinement of the process improves.

Initial Program Evaluation Planning

It is important that the composition of evaluation approaches for program package evaluation include the instructional, scheduling, financial, staffing, and support services impact upon the system for review prior to funding. A suggested form for this planning procedure is provided Exhibit 10.2.

Exhibit 10.2   Program Package Development Planning Form

I. Preliminary Planning and Communication Information:
Program name: _____ Package: _____
Submitted by: _____ Date: _____
School(s) affected by the program (list all and include the area):
1. Program Description and Goals Information: How many students and staff will benefit from the implementation of this program?
2. Needs Assessment Information: Why has this program been developed? (Include research base if appropriate and provide specific data to support the program.) How is the program linked to the district strategic plan?
II. Information about Development of the Program:
1. What other options were investigated? 2. Why was this option selected? What are its greatest benefits? 3. Who will handle the development, implementation, evaluation, and management of the program? 4. How will the program be staffed? (Describe present and new staff needs and costs). 5. List additional nonstaff costs for program implementation and source(s) of funds. 6. Describe the ongoing professional development needed to support the program. 7. Describe the impact on school scheduling and transportation (if any). 8. Who has been involved in the development of the program? 9. Describe the impact on curriculum and instruction. 10. How will the program component be evaluated?

The form in Exhibit 10.2 is useful (1) to assist program managers to organize information pertinent to the evaluation of program packages and (2) to provide members of the budget advisory team with information during the program manager's presentation to the team.

To facilitate responding to the questions in the form in Exhibit 10.2 above relative to evaluation, the questions that follow in Exhibit 10.3 might be of use to program managers.

Exhibit 10.3   Questions for Developing Program Package Evaluation

General Information:

1. What is the program to be evaluated?
   a. What are the objectives of the program package?
   b. How was the program package intended to affect student achievement?
2. What is the cost of the program package?
3. What problems have been encountered in implementing the program package?
4. How does the program package align with research literature?

Evaluative Information:

5. What questions need to be answered with the program package evaluation?
6. What methods will be used to collect data and why?
   a. What data will be collected?
   b. How will data be disaggregated by SES, gender, and ethnicity?
   c. Will data collection procedures enable indentifying strengths and weaknesses?
7. What is the timeline for completion of the evaluation?
8. What staff are involved in program implementation?
9. How will data from the evaluation be used?
10. Will data collection procedures produce ways and means for program improvement?

Reporting Findings:

11. How will findings be reported? If not written, why?
   a. How will the data provided be used to improve student achievement?
   b. What recommendations are planned based upon the data and results?

Following the development of an evaluation plan for program packages, the budget process proceeds with the priority determinations as described earlier. However, it is advisable for the system to require a follow-up to program package implementation, which includes a summative or cumulative analysis of the results from the program package implementation.

Exhibit 10.4 provides a format for summative evaluation after a semester or two of implementation of the program component.

As a rule, evaluation reports need to be succinct and focused on key information needed to determine the efficacy of the program and areas for improvement. An executive summary is helpful for administrators and governing boards to get an accurate, but concise, picture of the program's results.

For administrators and governing boards to make a determination regarding program effectiveness and further funding, the evaluation report should foster the capability to answer the following questions.

- How effective was the program in accomplishing its purposes?
- How has the program or its various components affected the quality of the school system and the accomplishment of its goals and objectives?

Exhibit 10.4   Suggested Summative Evaluation Report Format

Program Name: _____ **Program Manager:** _____

Program Information:

How long has the program been in place?

What has the funding been for this program over the past three years?

Number of students involved: _____ Number of staff involved: _____

Strategic plan strategies and action plans addressed by this program:

Specific Program Results Information:

1. What are the goals and objectives of the program?

2. What are the program's distinctive characteristics, activities, and services?

3. How would these particular activities enable the program to reach its goals?

4. What factors relating to increased student achievement were used to assess the program? *(Include quantitative and qualitative measures, disaggregated by SES, gender, and ethnicity).*

5. What indicators of program effectiveness (including student achievement) were used to assess the quality of the program?

6. Was the program implemented as planned? How was it modified and/or adjusted over time?

7. Was the program differentially effective with particular types of participants?

8. Prepare and include a chart comparing projected and actual costs of the program.

9. Summarize the program's overall findings including strengths and areas to improve.

10. Present any recommendations for future consideration of this program.

- How does the program work, what does it cost, and what value does it provide?
- Should this program be modified, continued, expanded, or terminated?

The preceding questions get at the heart of assuring greater quality in program design and implementation. Many programs are initiated in school systems because of some key person's interest in or acquaintance with an intervention. However, at the start, many of these programs fail to have clearly defined objectives and goals, with an accompanying strategy that can effectively evaluate results of the intervention to see if it is worth its cost.

It's clear that school systems need to carefully select programs that are aligned to the systems needs, goals, and objectives. Moreover, evaluation of programs and packages is essential if the school system is to improve the quality of its operations, services, and results. Without sound and valid evaluation structures and procedures in place, the system is not able to make the essential decisions it needs to make for an exemplary and high-quality school system deserving community support, adequate funding, and community pride.

Evaluating the Process

Performance-based budgeting is built on a philosophical framework that requires the following components in the school system's operations and activities for adoption of a new program:

- A clear understanding of the needs of the system that can be served by the intervention
- Determination of the program intervention's objectives and their alignment with system goals
- A robust grasp of how the program intervention is going to work, with professional training provided to support successful execution of the program
- A well-designed system for evaluating the results of the program intervention

Any program must be subjected to evaluation as to its suitability and the results it demonstrates congruently with the needs of the system. The performance-based budgeting program is not excluded from this requirement.

To assist school systems in evaluating the performance-based budgeting process itself, the evaluation instrument in Exhibit 10.5 is provided. It should be pointed out that the instrument should be administered as follows:

- Only members of the budget advisory team should complete the evaluation form.
- The form should be completed anonymously and collected in a confidential location.
- Scoring of the form should be completed by three or more members of the budget advisory team, working jointly.
- Results should be distributed to all members of the budget advisory team and to key administrative leaders and the governing board.

SUMMARY

In this chapter, the essentiality of evaluation of system operations and activities is presented, with the intention of providing the governing board and the system administration with tools for quality assurance and quality control. School systems are generally considered rational organizations with established goals and expectations that drive implementation of programs and activities of the system. To close the quality control loop, some means of determining whether or not the system achieved its intended goals and objectives is required—that is, through assessment and evaluation.

Evaluation needs to be timely, objective in nature, and valid in its design and procedure. End products of programmatic initiatives must be assessed for

(Text continues on page 151)

Exhibit 10.5   Budget Advisory Team Evaluation of Performance-Based Budgeting

Directions: This instrument is for evaluating the budget-making process that was used this year. Only members of the budget advisory team should complete this evaluation. Please read each item, and check the appropriate box with your response in the column at the right.

Response Key: D = Disagree with this statement
N = Neutral or no opinion on this statement
A = Agree with this statement

Example: Sample A shows how this rating scale works. If you agreed with the statement, you would mark as follows:

	D	N	A
Sample A. The amount of money was irrelevant in our planning.	☐	☐	■

Please respond with your opinion on each of the following items:

	D	N	A
1. I believe it is important to continue the performance-based budgeting process in our schools.	☐	☐	☐
2. The district's strategic plan and goals helped guide the budgeting decisions.	☐	☐	☐
3. Special interest or pressure groups had little effect on our budgeting decisions.	☐	☐	☐
4. The broad participation of stakeholders in our budget planning was beneficial and appropriate.	☐	☐	☐
5. Teachers and principals should continue to be included in priority setting for the final budget.	☐	☐	☐
6. The best options for our students were the greatest influence on the priorities of the budget.	☐	☐	☐
7. Feedback on performance and program results was used effectively to set budget priorities.	☐	☐	☐
8. Parents, board, teachers, or administrators didn't unduly influence funding for any programs.	☐	☐	☐
9. Information about program packages or components was sufficient to make sound judgments.	☐	☐	☐
10. The ranking of program components was reasonable and appropriate and I was comfortable with it.	☐	☐	☐
11. We should be able to change the ranking of packages *within* a program (now set by the program manager).	☐	☐	☐
12. It is important for even more people to have a voice in the district's budget priority-setting process.	☐	☐	☐
13. The district should go back to the previous budget-setting process without such broad participation.	☐	☐	☐

(Continued)

Exhibit 10.5 (Continued)

	D	N	A
14. The credibility of the school district will be better because of the performance-based budgeting approach.	☐	☐	☐
15. An outside facilitator is helpful in the priority-setting process, and needs to be continued.	☐	☐	☐

16. What did you find *most valuable* about the performance-based budgeting process?

17. What did you feel *could be improved* about the performance-based budgeting process?

18. What suggestions do you have for defining or describing the program areas differently?

19. Which of the following would be your preference for serving as the facilitator of the district performance-based budget meetings?
   ☐ Someone from outside the district   ☐ An in-district administrator   ☐ Other:

20. From your experience, what worked well during the development and preparation of budget packages? What would you change?

21. What worked well during the budget advisory team deliberations?

22. How would you change the district budget committee deliberations?

23. Additional comments:

Please indicate the group you represented on the budget planning committee:
☐ Teacher   ☐ Parent   ☐ Community Member   ☐ Administrator   ☐ Other: ____

My overall level of satisfaction: ☐ Very High   ☐ High   ☐ O.K.   ☐ Low   ☐ Very Low

---

Thank you for completing this questionnaire. Please return or mail it in to the budgeting office.

effect and character (summative evaluation), but progress during implementation needs to be monitored as well (formative evaluation). Policies of the system need to contain specific information that prescribes these important elements of evaluation.

Moreover, policies also need to prescribe the requirements for program proposals before implementation to assure that measurable objectives are delineated, effective practices are planned, financial prerequisites are available, and results are measurable and informative for decision making as to the viability and value of the initiative.

Once evaluation systems are in place and performance-based budgeting commences, the budgeting process itself needs to be evaluated for suitability within the organization. Suggested guidelines for effectuating the evaluation structures have been outlined within this chapter.

Of course, the impact and effect of the budget development process hinges upon the actual budget itself. It is important for the governing board and chief executive officer of the system to examine the final product and determine if the newly constructed budget and format meet expectations and goals for the system. Some guidelines for this task are provided in the next chapter.

11

Ideas to Action

Budgeting at times may appear as "mission impossible." Given fewer resources than needed to carry out the responsibilities of the system, the situation isn't always hopeless. In that case, the system leadership needs to question revenue and expenditure assumptions, history, projections, mandates, the "musts," and the continuing costs. As one Montana school board member stated, "We can't get ten pounds of sugar out of a five pound sack." The system needs to think outside the box and find ways and means to change policies and approaches to boost revenues and/or reduce expenditures. Rolling current activities forward into successive years without careful scrutiny of results will continue to suboptimize system improvement. The principle of abandonment helps here—if it isn't possible to support all system responsibilities, something has to go. If additional resources can be found and secured, then additional responsibilities can be reinstituted.

COMPLETING THE JOURNEY

To make performance-based budgeting work effectively, governing boards and administrators need to gain useful knowledge about educational and learning needs of the system, resources available, options and alternatives for delivery of programs and services, and how to improve quality within financial limitations and constraints. In order to make a difference in the educational system, the organization needs to move to higher, more profound types of budgeting practice to make data-driven decisions.

Gone are the days of relying on "rollover" types of budgeting and enrollment-driven allocations, which build upon prior allocations and fail to account for the dramatic differences among clientele and individual schools. The challenge is to organize and implement a budgeting system to improve student performance significantly. See Appendix D in the back of the book for the story of one school system that made performance-based budgeting work to build public confidence.

It is possible, and perhaps even necessary, to use accurate system information to enhance the achievement of all students by understanding student progress and program performance (Cokins & Pirrello, 2007). Performance-based budgeting addresses a number of issues to help school systems shift from historical allocation systems to a framework of information and action to improve performance of the system at all levels. Some of these issues and challenges are discussed below.

BUDGET ISSUES AND CHALLENGES

Several issues and challenges face school systems, including those in the following sections.

Adequacy

Historically, school budgeting has been replete with anomalies. For example, budget requests and mandates have frequently exceeded available resources. Coupled with economic limitations, schools have often been placed in the position of reducing expenditures; but at the same time, demands for improved quality have emerged. Reconciling the two conflicting best interests has been thorny at best.

Regrettably, funding and financial resources for public school systems have not gained a high priority among policy makers, legislators, and other authorities. Public school funding options meet resistance, and in some cases become an emotional flashpoint within the community (Potts, 2002).

Funding for improvement efforts and new initiatives in pupil achievement, if it is to come, may largely come from current resources. Finding where and how to reallocate current funding from lower to higher priorities may be served well with performance-based-budgeting approaches.

Relevancy

Relevant and practicable connections between performance or results and program expenditures traditionally have been tenuous or often nonexistent. The need is for discernment obtained from analysis of assessment and performance data on programs and services to understand how various initiatives are reaching successful learner and organizational performance. Budgeting processes have seldom focused on results of programs, goals, and feedback.

Relevant and appropriate budgeting processes need to provide the means to measure program effectiveness and student progress to avoid waste and inefficiency.

Performance-based budgeting goes a long way toward this goal by using longitudinal data to identify trends and patterns that guide more astute decision making in the allocation process.

Practice and Priority

One of the major thrusts in budgeting normally is quality improvement. Research writings have indicated that participatory decision making with stakeholders strengthens understanding, builds commitment, and enhances the quality of decision making (Deming, 1986). It also goes without saying that the better the information provided in budgeting about performance and cost-effectiveness, the better the decisions that may be made.

The net result of scarcity in resource availability is that some budget requests may not be funded. This is true at all levels and in all types of budgeting. Some things have to be left out if there isn't sufficient money to fund them. The dilemma of how to determine what to fund or to not fund is resolved in performance-based budgeting with priority setting.

Priorities enable the allocation of scarce or limited resources on programs demonstrating the most importance to and the most critical effect on the main mission of the system—pupil learning.

Implementation

Productivity of the school system depends upon a budget that supplies clear, tangible connections between program objectives, costs, and measured results. As results improve with the same or even diminishing resources, the greater productivity improves. In the vernacular, more "bang from the buck" describes productivity imperatives. Implementing performance-based budgeting increases the likelihood that productivity can get better.

The credibility of the school system budget depends upon how well the allocations are understood, how the monies are used efficiently, and how effectively system quality improves. Given convincing assessment information, a focus on performance results, collaborative decision making, and the application of appropriate allocations in priority order, system efficacy becomes apparent over time. The quality improvement loop becomes closed, and the alignment of goals, program activities, and performance evaluation approaches unity.

PRODUCTIVITY: RAISING PERFORMANCE OVER TIME WITHIN FINANCIAL LIMITS

Productivity just doesn't happen. It goes beyond historical procedures to appropriate actions and data-driven decisions to increase the certainty that budget decisions will lead to improvement. Naturally, there is a big difference between formulating a strategy and making it work. Performance-based budgeting involves identifying opportunities for improvement across the entire spectrum of programs and services in the system, selecting activities and allocating funds accordingly, and then making decisions that move toward quality improvement.

Quality improvement is a continuous, systemwide framework, not a onetime analysis or event. Its goal is to optimize the performance of both the entire organization and individual students.

Optimizing the system requires unity in focusing on the system's aims and purposes, and in avoiding the improvement of one program to the detriment of another, thus undermining overall organizational performance. Some people consider "optimization" difficult, if not impossible, to achieve. However, governance and leadership is about being practical, not theoretical. The key is to synchronize the organizational priorities to constantly move in the right direction with sound and meaningful information. Historically, competition for resources within a system's allocation processes subverts organizational harmony by failing to use performance data and goal orientation in budget decision making. The political nature of historical funding patterns has no place in a quality-centered organization.

Performance-based budgeting evolves from closely held allocation processes to a data-driven, high-visibility, transparent, and collaborative process to determine decisions and actions for improving performance across the board for students and schools.

Building System Productivity

Performance-based budgeting is similar to activity accounting in the private sector. The performance-based-budget process is simply a method of measuring the cost and performance of activities against the system's goals and objectives. The process organizes programs into separate, but connected as incremental pieces of the whole, cost units with corresponding activities and functions within each cost unit (package). In effect, the goal-based program drives the budgetary unit cost, rather than the other way around (English, 1987).

Governing boards and administrative leaders usually determine the organizational structure of programs and program subunits, or packages. The primary task of performance-based budgeting is to break programs down into ascending levels of quality, starting from a base level set by policy, which can then considered in relationship to other program packages in a priority-setting process.

Program package costs reside in resources, which are such things as material, personnel, space, equipment, technology, utilities, and services. Each program subunit level of activity needs to have a unit of measure that is useful and effective in determining the value and benefit of the program unit at the specific cost level.

There is no one way to proceed with improving system productivity; but it may be approached as a continuous improvement project, with the budget being developed by adding incremental program subunits (packages) until the resulting incremental improvements and costs exceed the maximum amount of revenue available or anticipated.

From a practical view, performance-based budgeting institutionalizes a flexible budgeting process with clear ties between the cost of a program subunit or package and the observable assessed result, which enables the system to fund packages based on value derived and comparisons with other packages.

Precursors of Productivity

School systems that exhibit improving productivity display some important attributes that undergird quality development. Some of these important attributes of system productivity enhancement reflect the following practices:

1. *Identification of specific aims, purposes, goals, and objectives.* Before school systems grab the cutting knife, they need to carefully identify what it is they hope to accomplish and how they are going to decide what best fits their intended purpose.

2. *Institutionalization of system commitment to improvement.* High quality school systems develop and implement plans for interventions to improve the performance of the system, with corresponding feedback on effectiveness and costs.

3. *Allocations driven by system and clientele needs.* Congruity between where the money goes and where the needs are in the system is highly valued and honored in budgeting processes. "One size fits all" is inequitable and unreasonable.

4. *Use of assessment information for decisions.* Specific means to attain better results over time are imbedded in policy, and valid and reliable data are used to guide decision making in process and at culmination of activities.

5. *Manifestations of businesslike atmosphere.* Environments mirror effective factors and characteristics of educational practice, advantageous student opportunities, healthful surroundings and facilities, and harmonious relationships.

6. *Organizational relationships support continuing improvement.* Teachers and principals participate in development of budget allocations, and principals have discretion in use of resources with accountability to system standards and expectations.

7. *Resources made available for system improvement.* School systems simply cannot hope to improve without important organizational elements including curriculum design and delivery, assessment systems, and professional development.

These attributes create a foundation for system productivity, which calls for progress in quality improvement over time with the same or fewer resources.

Governing boards and school leaders need to recognize these strong and critical factors if the system is ever to achieve excellence.

IMPLEMENTING ACTION AND ACHIEVING RESULTS

The approach to modify budget processes normally takes three to five years to fully implement. Discerning school leaders know full well that change cannot be mandated from the top down and that all change is a journey, not a blueprint (Fullan, 1993). There is a substantial paradigm shift in the relationship between costs and programs, which calls for the mission of the system to drive the budget and not the other way around (English, 1987).

Instead of first looking at revenues and deciding what will be "allowed," the performance-based budgeting process starts with goals and objectives, determination of program priorities, diagnosed needs, and feedback on performance; then it moves to allocations to meet the needs and accomplish the goals. It is usually advisable for a system to begin the change process by tying it to the development and adoption of a system long-range plan that articulates what the system wishes to accomplish. Resources then are means to the ends (goals).

A simplistic metaphor that exemplifies this phenomenon is found in garment production. A producer of a garment selects a pattern, determines how much fabric is needed, and then obtains the fabric to construct the garment. On the other hand, if the producer were following a customary model of budgeting, he or she would first obtain an indeterminate amount of fabric (the "revenues"), and begin constructing a garment according to the pattern—stopping when the fabric is expended, regardless of how much of the pattern had been completed. In effect, the latter example is "cutting the pattern to fit the cloth," instead of the other way around. In school budgeting, it is not unusual for the budget revenues to manipulate the programs and services of the system.

There are two considerations and structures germane to performance-based budgeting: (1) program development criteria and (2) essential components of the program-based budget.

The first of these considerations, development of programs and services that are congruent with a rational organizational approach to quality, entails adherence to a specific number of criteria. The criteria suggested are delineated here:

1. A formal plan, with measurable goals and objectives and designed procedures is in place.

2. Staff proficiencies needed to implement the plan are clearly defined.

3. Program initiatives are developed for implementation of the plan.

4. Personnel, material, and financial resources needed for program initiatives are identified and available.

5. Goals, objectives, and expectations are systematically evaluated.

6. Responsibilities and procedures for monitoring implementation of programs are identified and assigned.

7. Modifications and adjustments in program design are responsive to evaluation feedback.

The second set of considerations is comprised of the essential components of a performance-based budget and the degree of adequacy found in their application and use. These components are defined below (Poston, 1992):

1. Tangible, demonstrable connections are evident between assessment of operational program effectiveness and allocations of resources.

2. Program components are rank ordered to permit flexibility in budget expansion, reduction, or stabilization based upon changing needs or priorities.

3. Each budget request or submittal is described in a manner that facilitates evaluation of consequences of funding, or not funding, in terms of performance or results.

4. Cost benefits of programs and services are incorporated in budget decision making and presented for consideration by the budget development group.

5. Budget requests and program subunits compete for funding based upon a collaborative process that evaluates criticality of need and efficacy in achievement of effectiveness.

6. Priorities and recommended allocations in the budget are established in participatory decision-making processes comprised of key system stakeholders, including teachers and principals.

With system commitment to and implementation of performance-based budgeting, the governing board and chief executive officer will be leading the school system on a journey toward educational excellence and renewed confidence in the improvement of organizational performance and quality.

It's a journey that is well worth taking.

Appendix A

BUILDING A BUDGET MANAGEMENT SYSTEM

Recommended Actions for Governing Boards and Superintendents

The following recommendations are typical of those proposed to school systems following curriculum management audits, in the event of audit findings that have traditional budgeting processes and that do not meet the criteria for performance-based budgeting. The recommendations proffer a fundamental set of actions to help a school system design and implement a budget planning process that is more programmatic in focus, includes strategies for effectively prioritizing expenditures, and tightens the linkage between resources and results.

To assist the system in clarifying responsibilities for the governing board and the administration, the recommended actions are divided into two parts: governance functions and administrative functions.

Governance Functions

The following actions are commonly recommended for governing boards (CMSi, 2009):

1. Instruct the superintendent to draft clearly worded policies regarding budget development and resource decision making that delineate expectations of processes that link the budget to plans, priorities, and needs that are based on data (expectations for the process are stated in Chapter 11). In conjunction with the superintendent, incorporate a preplanning step in which the superintendent and board identify and articulate the priorities and goals around which the system budget should be developed.

2. Adopt a policy or policies that describe system expectations for the budgeting system (see policy requirements in Chapter 5) and direct implementation of the policy with the next budget planning cycle, starting in incremental steps to be described in administrative procedures.

3. Make board-level decisions congruent with the intent of the newly adopted policies, requiring data-driven recommendations that have been through preliminary prioritizing based on the criteria in the policy, the district and school planning, and reiterated by the governing board and superintendent prior to beginning budget development. (Ensure that systemwide stakeholder participation has been incorporated into the various planning goals and priorities that are used as the foundation for decisions.)

4. Allow three to five years for full implementation of the revised approach to performance-based budget development. Request recommendations for refinements as needed throughout the implementation phase.

Administrative Functions

The following actions are frequently recommended to the school system superintendent of schools:

1. Draft a proposed policy or policies for performance-based budget management for the governing board. Following adoption of board policy, develop administrative procedures for the implementation of budget development procedural changes to accompany and implement the policy. With the chief financial officer, develop steps and forms that reflect the intended changes and methods of organizing information for budget decision making.

2. Determine with the board the various levels of desired participation in budget development, the package levels desired, and the structure of the decision-making process, and implement accordingly.

3. Incorporate the change process associated with performance-based budgeting in steps over the next three years. In general, the process may be designed to work as follows:

   a. Initiate financial forecasting procedures to project financial, enrollment, and operational changes and situations anticipated for the next three to five years.

   b. Commence identification of various educational activities or programs and group them into broad areas of need or purposes served. Structure program units such as elementary instruction, kindergarten, English language learning, special education, gifted education, district governance, superintendent's office, financial services, warehousing, personnel services, fine arts, athletics, food services, staff development, specific programs or interventions, and so on. Divide the organization into the most logical subgroups possible based on the existing operating structure. For the first year, the program units could even be fewer in number, such as a cluster of curricular offerings, multischool programs, or similar program units. Seek to establish 15 to 25 programmatic units initially.

   c. Build subunits within programs, with incremental "packages" within each of the program units by the priority with which they deliver the need or purpose. For example, any given program could be defined and subdivided into units, or packages, which provide programs and services at various levels of quality:

  i. Basic or "recovery" packages: One or more increments that characterize what the program would be like with less funding than the previous year (90%, 95%, etc.).

  ii. Current or existing package: What the program would be like given the same funding level as the previous year (100%).

  iii. Enhancement packages: One or more increments that characterize what the program would be like with greater funding than the previous year (101% or more). These program subunits or packages may differ from year to year as the process becomes more sophisticated and data driven.

d. Prepare guidelines and recommended steps for program managers for guidance in developing program units (see Chapter 7).

e. Instruct the designated program directors and managers to prepare concise and meaningful budget packages for their areas with each package representing a level of activity that stands alone but builds sequentially on the previous year's package.

f. Request inclusion of a goal statement for each program area or budget package that states the program purpose, its criteria for success, and how it will be evaluated. Each budget request shall be described to permit evaluation of the consequences of funding or nonfunding in terms of student performance results. Require cost-to-benefit analysis in this procedure.

  i. Compile goal statements and budget packages and share with appropriate staff to gather data that best describe service levels, program outcomes at each level of funding, and cost benefits.

  ii. Define organizational performance data with the appropriate involvement of staff (including principals, teachers, and support staff), current and desired service levels, and program objectives. Require that building and program assessment data be used in the development of budgets.

  iii. Compile historical cost information, especially expenditure percentages of budget, with program performance data and recommendations to guide preliminary budget-building estimates.

g. Organize and convene a budget advisory team to include stakeholders such as centralized district administrators, parent groups, employee associations, citizen committees, and site councils for the purpose of developing the budget proposal collaboratively. Budget requests need to compete with each other for funding based upon evaluation of priority of need and level of program effectiveness.

h. Instruct the budget advisory team to evaluate and rank budget program packages and take responsibility for recommending a rank-ordered budget to the superintendent, who in turn reviews and makes the final recommendation to the board.

i. The superintendent initiates final compilation of the budget components. After reviewing the results of the budget advisory team's work, the superintendent directs that the tentative budget is published with program components/packages listed in priority order for board consideration.

j. The governing board accordingly proceeds to review the tentative budget, and to receive presentations of information about each program request, usually in a study session. Following the data presentations, the board evaluates the tentative budget program package rankings and establishes the final configuration of the budget for official approval and implementation. Remaining parts of the budget, such as construction, capital outlay, and other fund accounts are then assembled within the total budget for public presentation and board final approval.

k. Capital outlay and improvement budgets, which may not be recurring cost centers, are recommended to be built from a "zero base" each fiscal year.

   i. Long range planning may promote multiyear planning for improvements, including life-cycle replacement and preventive maintenance.

   ii. Prioritization should be based on health, safety, and impact on the learning environment and protection of investment.

   iii. Many capital funding needs change annually and do not reoccur once met and paid for, such as durable goods and construction costs. The budget planning process should reflect these changes while projecting life-cycle replacement costs over five to ten years.

l. Once the budget configuration is finalized and the board has approved the final budget, budget allocations are based on revenues available; the appropriation levels to be authorized; and program funding priorities, rankings, and recommendation as authorized by the board.

m. With the prioritized listing of request packages in place, the "cutoff line" can be drawn when the more precise revenue projection is finalized. In effect, the budget limit may be clearly designated in the rank-ordered list of program packages, subject to modification in the event that available revenues increase or decrease over time.

n. The budget, as authorized by the board, is set in place and commences execution under supervision of the superintendent.

4. Retain within the role of the superintendent the oversight of financial decision making, along with the responsibility for overseeing the mission of the school system. This ensures a comprehensive view of the system as well as connectivity and congruity among program, budget, and facility planning.

Continuation for Subsequent Budget Cycles

Once the process has been implemented and evaluated, the superintendent may increase the application of the revised budget development steps annually until all system budgeting follows similar performance-based budgeting procedures. Refine and modify as needed to accomplish the goal of a data-driven decision-making framework and an allocation system based upon measured needs, essentiality to the system, and monitored results. In this manner, the school system's quest for quality will persevere and endure.

Appendix B

Needs Assessment of Budget Policy and Development Issues

Name:_____ Position: _____

School District: _____ Date: _____

	Strongly Agree	Agree	No Opinion	Disagree	Strongly Disagree
1. Collaborative decisions are preferred in budget building.	☐	☐	☐	☐	☐
2. School units must have autonomy and flexibility in using allocated resources within their unit.	☐	☐	☐	☐	☐
3. District allocations per student must be provided dissimilarly in accordance with differing needs of students.	☐	☐	☐	☐	☐
4. Membership of the budget decision-making team must be broad and comprehensive, involving the following stakeholders:					
a. Teachers	☐	☐	☐	☐	☐
b. Support Employees	☐	☐	☐	☐	☐
c. Parents and Citizens	☐	☐	☐	☐	☐
d. Business Community	☐	☐	☐	☐	☐
e. Financial Advisory Groups	☐	☐	☐	☐	☐
f. Students	☐	☐	☐	☐	☐
g. Principals	☐	☐	☐	☐	☐
h. Board Members	☐	☐	☐	☐	☐

(Continued)

(Continued)

	Strongly Agree	Agree	No Opinion	Disagree	Strongly Disagree
5. Budget priorities must be set by participation of key stakeholders.	☐	☐	☐	☐	☐
6. Budget priorities should be connected to district goals, objectives, and planning.	☐	☐	☐	☐	☐
7. Budget requests must be made in terms of clearly defined program areas with all costs identified and included.	☐	☐	☐	☐	☐
8. Tangible connections must be evident between assessments of performance and program allocations.	☐	☐	☐	☐	☐
9. Program requests must be rank-ordered in order of importance to the district.	☐	☐	☐	☐	☐
10. Program requests must be stated incrementally and reflecting reduction, stabilization, and expansion options.	☐	☐	☐	☐	☐
11. Budget procedures should reflect short- and long-range planning.	☐	☐	☐	☐	☐
12. The budget format must provide program options to obtain the greatest educational returns in the most cost-efficient manner.	☐	☐	☐	☐	☐
13. Funding sources should include all practical and legal funding options.	☐	☐	☐	☐	☐
14. If resources are insufficient to fund district priorities, additional support should be sought from the community, including district taxpayers.	☐	☐	☐	☐	☐
15. Assessment data must be used to establish budget priorities.	☐	☐	☐	☐	☐
16. Budget requests for individual programs must include all costs for delivery of activities and services.	☐	☐	☐	☐	☐
17. Knowledge of results and performance of programs must be used in determining program needs.	☐	☐	☐	☐	☐
18. Program needs must be expressed as budget requests.	☐	☐	☐	☐	☐
19. Annually developed budgeting objectives should become a basic factor in the budget allocation process.	☐	☐	☐	☐	☐
20. Purposes for use of resources must be established at the board level, and plans for use of resources must be established at the school and program level.	☐	☐	☐	☐	☐

Appendix C

Summary of Program Evaluation Standards[1]

PROPRIETY STANDARDS

The propriety standards are intended to ensure that an evaluation will be conducted legally, ethically, and with due regard for the welfare of those involved in the evaluation, as well as those affected by its results.

P1: Service Orientation. Evaluations should be designed to assist organizations to address and effectively serve the needs of the full range of targeted participants.

P2: Formal Agreements. Obligations of the formal parties to an evaluation (what is to be done, how, by whom, when) should be agreed to in writing, so that these parties are obligated to adhere to all conditions of the agreement or formally to renegotiate it.

P3: Rights of Human Subjects. Evaluations should be designed and conducted to respect and protect the rights and welfare of human subjects.

P4: Human Interactions. Evaluators should respect human dignity and worth in their interactions with other persons associated with an evaluation, so that participants are not threatened or harmed.

P5: Complete and Fair Assessment. The evaluation should be complete and fair in its examination and recording of strengths and weaknesses of the program being evaluated, so that strengths can be built upon and problem areas addressed.

P6: Disclosure of Findings. The formal parties to an evaluation should ensure that the full set of evaluation findings along with pertinent limitations are made accessible to the persons affected by the evaluation and any others with expressed legal rights to receive the results.

---

[1]Joint Committee on Standards for Educational Evaluation, Sanders, J., Chair. (1994). *Program evaluation standards.* Retrieved from: http://www.jcsee.org/program-evaluation-standards

P7: Conflict of Interest. Conflict of interest should be dealt with openly and honestly, so that it does not compromise the evaluation processes and results.

P8: Fiscal Responsibility. The evaluator's allocation and expenditure of resources should reflect sound accountability procedures and otherwise be prudent and ethically responsible, so that expenditures are accounted for and appropriate.

UTILITY STANDARDS

The utility standards are intended to ensure that an evaluation will serve the information needs of intended users.

U1: Stakeholder Identification. Persons involved in or affected by the evaluation should be identified, so that their needs can be addressed.

U2: Evaluator Credibility. The persons conducting the evaluation should be both trustworthy and competent to perform the evaluation, so that the evaluation findings achieve maximum credibility and acceptance.

U3: Information Scope and Selection. Information collected should be broadly selected to address pertinent questions about the program and be responsive to the needs and interests of clients and other specified stakeholders.

U4: Values Identification. The perspectives, procedures, and rationale used to interpret the findings should be carefully described, so that the bases for value judgments are clear.

U5: Report Clarity. Evaluation reports should clearly describe the program being evaluated, including its context, and the purposes, procedures, and findings of the evaluation, so that essential information is provided and easily understood.

U6: Report Timeliness and Dissemination. Significant interim findings and evaluation reports should be disseminated to intended users, so that they can be used in a timely fashion.

U7: Evaluation Impact. Evaluations should be planned, conducted, and reported in ways that encourage follow-through by stakeholders, so that the likelihood that the evaluation will be used is increased.

FEASIBILITY STANDARDS

The feasibility standards are intended to ensure that an evaluation will be realistic, prudent, diplomatic, and frugal.

F1: Practical Procedures. The evaluation procedures should be practical, to keep disruption to a minimum while needed information is obtained.

F2: Political Viability. The evaluation should be planned and conducted with anticipation of the different positions of various interest groups, so that their cooperation may be obtained, and so that possible attempts by any of these groups to curtail evaluation operations or to bias or misapply the results can be averted or counteracted.

F3: Cost Effectiveness. The evaluation should be efficient and produce information of sufficient value, so that the resources expended can be justified.

ACCURACY STANDARDS

The accuracy standards are intended to ensure that an evaluation will reveal and convey technically adequate information about the features that determine worth or merit of the program being evaluated.

A1: Program Documentation. The program being evaluated should be described and documented clearly and accurately, so that the program is clearly identified.

A2: Context Analysis. The context in which the program exists should be examined in enough detail, so that its likely influences on the program can be identified.

A3: Described Purposes and Procedures. The purposes and procedures of the evaluation should be monitored and described in enough detail, so that they can be identified and assessed.

A4: Defensible Information Sources. The sources of information used in a program evaluation should be described in enough detail, so that the adequacy of the information can be assessed.

A5: Valid Information. The information-gathering procedures should be chosen or developed and then implemented so that they will assure that the interpretation arrived at is valid for the intended use.

A6: Reliable Information. The information-gathering procedures should be chosen or developed and then implemented so that they will assure that the information obtained is sufficiently reliable for the intended use.

A7: Systematic Information. The information collected, processed, and reported in an evaluation should be systematically reviewed, and any errors found should be corrected.

A8: Analysis of Quantitative Information. Quantitative information in an evaluation should be appropriately and systematically analyzed so that evaluation questions are effectively answered.

A9: Analysis of Qualitative Information. Qualitative information in an evaluation should be appropriately and systematically analyzed so that evaluation questions are effectively answered.

A10: Justified Conclusions. The conclusions reached in an evaluation should be explicitly justified, so that stakeholders can assess them.

A11: Impartial Reporting. Reporting procedures should guard against distortion caused by personal feelings and biases of any party to the evaluation, so that evaluation reports fairly reflect the evaluation findings.

A12: Metaevaluation. The evaluation itself should be formatively and summatively evaluated against these and other pertinent standards, so that its conduct is appropriately guided and, on completion, stakeholders can closely examine its strengths and weaknesses.

Appendix D

Editorial in Reference to Performance-Based Budgeting

During school year 1994–95, Dr. Larry Vaughn, superintendent of the Wichita, Kansas, schools, prepared his system for a major change in budgeting. After over a year of professional development, budget process reconfigurations, and considerable work by a budget advisory team, Dr. Vaughn publicly presented the refurbished budget format, containing collaboratively developed rank-ordered program package components. The local press discussed the innovative approach to the system's budget in an editorial shortly after the new budget presentation.

The Wichita Eagle

Saturday, June 24, 1995   Page 8A

'Getting' it

Wichita school leaders hear, respond to critics

To all the folks hereabouts who have had a field day pointing out the shortcomings of the Wichita school district during the past few years: The school district "gets" it now.

All it takes to sense that there's been a fundamental change in the culture of the school district is a glance at the budget document made public by the district this week. Titled, appropriately, "1995–96 Proposed Budget . . . At a Glance," the document is a marvel of clarity and simplicity. The dense, confusing district budget books of the past are no more.

(Continued)

171

(Continued)

Just as important, the document makes clear that Superintendent Larry Vaughn and his staff understand that they must squeeze—really squeeze—every available dollar to continue to deliver schooling to the children of Wichita. In response to the voters' rejection of last year's local option budget, to a small decline in enrollment and an anticipated decrease in local property tax revenue due to a change in federal mortgage regulations, the school district has slashed its payroll by a net of 80 employees, while *increasing* the number of teachers in classrooms by nine.

Of the Wichita district's proposed $255.8 million budget, nearly $185 million—72%—will go to instruction and instructional support. Another 20% will go to such operations as busing, heating and cooling of school buildings, security, food service, maintenance, and data processing. And only $9.3 million—not nearly enough—will go to capital improvements on the district's 100 buildings.

The proposal probably is not perfect, which is why the Wichita school board and the public will have a chance to make any changes perceived to be necessary between now and August, when final budget approval is due. But Mr. Vaughn and his budgeting staff deserve great credit not only for hearing the complaints of the district's critics, but for responding to the them—in a way that ensures schoolchildren come first.

References

Foreword

Bourdieu, P. (1998). *Acts of resistance: Against the tyranny of the market* (R. Nice, Trans). New York: New Press.

Keyes, R. (1995). *The wit and wisdom of Harry Truman.* New York: Gramercy Books.

Chapter 1

Barr, R. B., & Tagg, J. (1995, November/December). From teaching to learning—A new paradigm for undergraduate education. *Change Magazine,* 13–25.

Deming, W. (1986). *Out of the crisis.* Cambridge, MA: Massachusetts Institute of Technology Press.

English, F. W. (1987). *Curriculum management for schools, colleges, business.* Springfield, IL: Charles C Thomas.

Mohrman, S., & Wohlstetter, P. (1994). *School-based management: Promise and process.* New Brunswick, NJ: Consortium for Policy Research in Education. Retrieved from http://www.cpre.org/images/stories/cpre_pdfs/fb05.pdf

Robinson, G. (1986). *Learning expectancy: A force changing education* (pamphlet). Washington, DC: Educational Research Service.

Schwartz, R. (1997). *Perspectives on educational policy research: Meeting the information needs of education policy makers.* Washington DC: The National Institute on Educational Governance, Finance, Policymaking, and Management. Office of Educational Research and Improvement. U.S. Department of Education.

Chapter 2

Berman, S., Davis, P., Koufman-Frederick, A., & Urion, D. (2001, March). *The impact of special education reform.* Retrieved from http://www.massupt.org/policy/fileDisplay.cfm?file=327

Bracey, G. (2008). Research: It's the same old song. *Phi Delta Kappan, 89*(6), 462–463.

Bushaw, W., & McNee, J. Americans speak out: Are educators and policy makers listening? The 41st annual Phi Delta Kappa/Gallup poll of the public's attitudes toward the public schools. *Phi Delta Kappan, 91*(1), 8–23.

Deming, W. (1986). *Out of the crisis.* Cambridge, MA: Massachusetts Institute of Technology Press.

Deming, W. (1993). *The new economics for industry, government, education.* Cambridge, MA: Massachusetts Institute of Technology, Center for Advanced Engineering Study.

English, F., & Steffy, B. (2001). *Deep curriculum alignment: Creating a level playing field for all children on high stakes tests of educational accountability.* Lanham, MD: Scarecrow Press.

Frase, L., English, F., & Poston, W. (2000). *The curriculum management audit: Improving school quality.* Lanham, MD: Scarecrow Press.

Hummel-Rossi, B., & Ashdown, J. (2002). The state of cost-benefit and cost-effectiveness analyses in education. *Review of Educational Research, 72*(1), 1–30.

Jacobs, J. (2009, October 20). Ideas not given to legislators. *The Des Moines Register,* p. 1A.

Koch, B. (1995, July 24). Comments to the USD 259 Board of Education. Wichita, KS: Wichita Chamber of Commerce.

Levin, H., & McEwan, P. (2002). Cost effectiveness and educational policy. In H. Levin & P. McEwan (Eds.), *Cost effectiveness and educational policy: 2002 yearbook of the American Education Finance Association* (pp. 1–17). Larchmont, NY: Eye on Education.

Maher, C., & Skidmore, M. (2007, October). *Voter responses to efforts to exceed school district revenue limits: The case of Wisconsin 1993–2004.* Paper prepared for presentation at the 19th Annual Association for Budgeting and Financial Management Conference. Retrieved from http://www .cviog.uga.edu/services/research/abfm/maher.pdf

National Center for Educational Statistics. (2009). *Digest of educational statistics.* U.S. Department of Education. Retrieved from http://nces.ed.gov/programs/projections/projections2018/tables .asp#group6

Pomerantz, M. (1995). Economic confidence in public education. Address to the Iowa Board of Regents.

Poston, W. (2009). *Budgeting problems and issues. Performance-based budgeting: Enhancing quality of education in times of scarcity.* Participant training manual. Johnston, IA: Curriculum Management Systems.

Poston, W., & Anton, R. (2005, December). *Put your money where your mouth is.* Address to the annual conference of the California School Boards Association. Presentation #933–127. San Diego, CA.

Salisbury, D. (2003, September 8). *Private schools cost less than you may think.* Retrieved from http:// www.cato.org/pub_display.php?pub_id=3231

Chapter 3

Deming, W. (1986). *Out of the crisis.* Cambridge, MA: Massachusetts Institute of Technology Press.

Downey, C., Steffy, B., Poston, W., & English, F. (2009). *50 ways to close the achievement gap* (3rd ed.). Thousand Oaks, CA: Corwin.

Eng, L. (1991, December 31). Schools feel squeeze of doing more with less. *Los Angeles Times,* p. B7.

English, F. (1986). *Curriculum auditing.* Lancaster, PA: Technomic.

Frase, L., English, F., & Poston, W. (2000). *The curriculum management audit: Improving school quality.* London: Scarecrow Press.

Kaufman, R., Herman, J., & Watters, K. (1996). *Educational planning: Strategic, tactical, operational.* Lancaster, PA: Technomic.

Mintzberg, H. (1994). The rise and fall of strategic planning. New York: Free Press.

Poston, W. (1994). *Making governance work: Total quality education for school boards.* Thousand Oaks, CA: Corwin.

U.S. Department of Education, National Center for Education Statistics. (2008, April). *National public education financial survey: 1989–90 through 2005–06.* Washington, DC: Author.

Chapter 4

Chabotar, K. (1987). Problems and opportunities in school financial management: A consultant's perspective. *Urban Education, 22*(1), 3–18.

Högye, M. (2002). *Theoretical approaches to public budgeting.* Budapest, Hungary: Local Government and Public Service Reform Initiative. Retrieved from http://lgi.osi.hu/publications/2002/216/ 101-Theory.pdf

Howard, S. (1973). *Changing state budgeting.* Lexington, KY: Council of State Governments.

Marzano, R., Pickering, D., & Pollock, J. (2001). *Classroom instruction that works: Research-based strategies for increasing student achievement.* Alexandria, VA: Association for Supervision and Curriculum Development.

Mikesell, J. (1991). *Fiscal administration—Analysis and applications for the public sector.* Pacific Grove, CA: Brooks/Cole.

New York Assembly. (2009). Bill number A7002: An act to amend the legislative law, in relation to requiring unfunded mandate notations. Retrieved from http://www.open.nysenate.gov/legislation/api/1.0/html/bill/A7002

Rogers, B. (2007, January 14). Overburdened schools. *Prospect Magazine, 130.* Retrieved from http://www.prospectmagazine.co.uk/2007/01/overburdenedschools/

Starcevich, M. (1990). A study relating elaborative cognitive processing of the learning task and achievement in cooperative learning groups (Doctoral dissertation). Drake University, Des Moines, IA.

U.S. House of Representatives. (2006, August 10). *Impact of rising energy costs on small business.* Retrieved from http://www.house.gov/smbiz/Reports/ENERGY%20REPORT%202006.pdf

Wildavsky, A., & Caiden, N. (1997). *The new politics of the budgetary process* (3rd ed.). New York: Addison Wesley Longman.

Chapter 5

Bliss, S. (1978). *Zero-base budgeting: A management tool for school districts.* Chicago: Research Corporation of the Association of School Business Officials.

Downey, C., Steffy, B., Poston, W., & English, F. (2009). *50 ways to close the achievement gap* (3rd ed.). Thousand Oaks, CA: Corwin.

Dyer, P. (1992). Reading recovery: A cost-effectiveness and educational outcomes analysis. *ERS Spectrum, 10*(1), 10–19.

English, F. W. (1987). *Curriculum management for schools, colleges, business.* Springfield, IL: Charles C Thomas.

English, F., & Steffy, B. (2001). *Deep curriculum alignment: Creating a level playing field for all children on high stakes tests of educational accountability.* Lanham, MD: Scarecrow Press.

National Association of State Budget Officers. (1998). *Budget analyst training program.* Retrieved from www.nasbo.org/publications/PDFs/training_modules.pdf

National Center for Educational Statistics. (2004). *Financial accounting for local and state school systems: Handbook 2* (2d rev.). Retrieved from http://nces.ed.gov/pubs2004/h2r2/ch_3.asp#2

Petty, R., & Cacioppo, J. (1986). *Communication and persuasion: Central and peripheral routes to attitude change.* New York: Springer-Verlag.

Ross, K., & Levačić, R. (Eds.). (1999). *Needs-based resource allocation in education: Via formula funding of schools.* Paris: International Institute for Educational Planning; United Nations Educational, Scientific, and Cultural Organization (UNESCO).

Schick, R., DeMasi, M., & Green M. (1992). Factors predicting writing performance. In A. C. Purves (ed.), *The IEA study of written composition: Vol. II* (pp. 153–168). Oxford, England: Pergamon.

Chapter 6

Bushaw, W., & McNee, J. (2009). Americans speak out: Are educators and policy makers listening? The 41st annual Phi Delta Kappa/Gallup poll of the public's attitudes toward the public schools. *Phi Delta Kappan, 91*(1), 8–23.

Deming, W. E. (1986). *Out of the Crisis.* Cambridge, MA: Massachusetts Institute of Technology Press.

Deming, W. E. (2000). *The new economics for industry, government, education* (2nd ed.). Cambridge, MA: Massachusetts Institute of Technology Press.

National Center for Educational Statistics. (2003). *Financial accounting for local and state educational systems*. Washington, D.C.: U. S. Department of Education. Institute of Education Sciences. Retrieved from http://nces.ed.gov/pubs2004/h2r2/ch_6_6.asp

Poston, W. (1994). *Making governance work: Total quality education for school boards*. Thousand Oaks, CA: Corwin.

Chapter 7

Abu-Duhou, I., Downes, P., & Levačić, R. (1999). Component 1: Basic student allocation. In K. Ross, & R. Levačić (Eds.), *Needs-based resource allocation in education: Via formula funding of schools* (pp. 59–90). Paris: International Institute for Educational Planning; United Nations Educational, Scientific, and Cultural Organization.

Caldwell, B., Levačić, R., & Ross, K. (1999). The role of formula funding of schools in different educational policy contexts. In K. Ross, & R. Levačić (Eds.), *Needs-based resource allocation in education: Via formula funding of schools* (pp. 9–24). Paris: International Institute for Educational Planning; United Nations Educational, Scientific, and Cultural Organization.

Clark, C., & Toenjes, L. (1996). *Exploring alternatives for school-based funding. Selected papers in educational finance*. Washington, DC: National Center for Education Statistics. Retrieved from http://nces.ed.gov/pubs98/clark.pdf

Dewey, J. (1916). *Democracy and education*. Hazleton, PA: Pennsylvania State University, Electronic Classics Series, J. Manis, Ed. Retrieved from http://www2hn/psu.edu/faculty/jmanis/johndewey/dem&ed.pdf

Downey, C., Steffy, B., Poston, W., & English, F. (2009). *50 ways to close the achievement gap* (3rd ed.). Thousand Oaks, CA: Corwin.

Editorial: "Red tape snares school principals." (2003, November 23). *Christian Science Monitor*. Retrieved from http://www.csmonitor.com/2003/1126/p10s03-comv.html

English, F., & Steffy, B. (2001). *Deep curriculum alignment: Creating a level playing field for all children on high stakes tests of educational accountability*. Lanham, MD: Scarecrow Press.

Hill, P., & Ross, K. (1999). Component 3: Student supplementary educational needs. In K. Ross, & R. Levačić (Eds.), *Needs-based resource allocation in education: Via formula funding of schools* (pp. 91–119). Paris: International Institute for Educational Planning; United Nations Educational, Scientific, and Cultural Organization.

Kozol, J. (1991). *Savage inequalities: Children in America's schools*. New York, NY: Harper Collins.

Levačić, R. (1999). Case study 2: Formula funding of schools in England and Wales. In K. Ross, & R. Levačić (Eds.), *Needs-based resource allocation in education: Via formula funding of schools* (pp. 161–197). Paris: International Institute for Educational Planning; United Nations Educational, Scientific, and Cultural Organization.

Murnane, R., & Phillips, B. (1981). Learning by doing, vintage, and selection: Three pieces of the puzzle relating teaching experience and teaching performance. *Economics of Education Review, 1*(4), 453–465.

Odden, A., & Archibald, S. (2001). *Reallocating resources: How to boost student achievement without asking for more*. Thousand Oaks, CA: Corwin.

Parish, T., Harr, J., Anthony, J., Merickel, A., & Esra, P. (2003). *State special education finance systems, 1999–2000*. Palo Alto, CA: The Center for Special Education Finance (CSEF), American Institutes for Research (AIR). Retrieved from http://csef.air.org/publications/csef/state/statpart1.pdf

Poston, W. (1992). The equity audit in school reform: Building a theory for institutional research. *International Journal of Educational Reform, 1*(3), 235–241.

Roza, M., & McCormick, M. (2006). Where the money goes: District allocation practices harming high-poverty schools. *School Business Affairs, 72*(1), 6–10.

Chapter 8

McKeown, B., & Thomas, D. (1988). *Q methodology*. Quantitative Applications in the Social Sciences Series, No. 66. Newbury Park, CA: Sage.

Oklahoma Association of Municipal Attorneys v. State, 577 P.2d 1310 (Okla. 1978).

Poston, W., Stone, P., & Muther, C. (1992). *Making schools work: Practical management of support operations.* Successful Schools Series, No. 7. Newbury Park, CA: Corwin.

Schwing, A. (2006–2008). *The open meeting law reference for all 50 states: Open meeting laws 2d.* Sponsored by the International Municipal Lawyers Association. Anchorage, AK: Fathom. Retrieved from http://www.openmeetinglaws.com/index.html

South Africa Scouts. (2009). *Qualities of a good committee chairperson.* South Africa: ScoutWeb. Retrieved from http://www.scouting.org.za/resources/committee/GoodChairperson.pdf

Chapter 9

Center for Teaching and Learning. (2010). *Mathematics of voting.* Tuscaloosa, AL: University of Alabama. Retrieved from http://www.ctl.ua.edu/math103/Voting/mathemat.htm

Lingle, R., & Feinberg, T. (2005). *Parliamentary procedures: Interesting facts and tips.* Urbana-Champaign: University of Illinois Extension. Retrieved from http://urbanext.illinois.edu/lcr/procedure.cfm

McKeown, B., & Thomas, D. (1988). *Q methodology.* Quantitative Applications in the Social Sciences Series, No. 66. Newbury Park, CA: Sage.

Chapter 10

Broh, R. (1982). *Managing quality for higher profits.* New York: McGraw-Hill. Retrieved from http://mot.vuse.vanderbilt.edu/mt322/Whatis.htm

Curriculum Management Systems, Inc. (CMSi). (2009). *The curriculum management improvement model: Level 1 Audit Training Program Book 2. Program evaluation.* Johnston, IA: Author.

Deming, W. (1986). *Out of the crisis.* Cambridge, MA: Massachusetts Institute of Technology Press.

Deming, W. (1993). *The new economics for industry, government, education.* Cambridge, MA: Massachusetts Institute of Technology Press.

Joint Committee on Standards for Educational Evaluation (Sanders, J., Chair). (1994). *The program evaluation standards: How to assess evaluations of educational programs.* Thousand Oaks, CA: Sage.

Katzenbach, J., & Smith, D. (1994). *The wisdom of teams: Creating the high-performance organization.* New York: HarperCollins.

Scriven, M. (1967). *The methodology of evaluation.* Washington DC: American Educational Research Association.

Spear, S. (2009). *Chasing the rabbit: How market leaders outdistance the competition and how great companies can catch up and win.* New York: McGraw-Hill

Chapter 11

Cokins, G., & Pirrello, C. (2007). *Putting it all together: A unified approach to performance management* (White Paper). Cary, NC: SAS Institute, Inc. Retrieved from http://www.sas.com/offices/asiapacific/taiwan/images/gary_notes/putting_it.pdf

English, F. W. (1987). *Curriculum management for schools, colleges, business.* Springfield, IL: Charles C Thomas.

Fullan, M. (1993). *Change forces: Probing the depths of educational reform.* London: Falmer (Routledge).

Poston, W. (1992, June). In times of scarcity, let the curriculum drive your budget. *The School Administrator.* 69(6), 18–21.

Potts, J. (2002, March 18). Public school funding options meet resistance. *Pittsburgh Tribune Review.* Retrieved from http://www.pittsburghlive.com/x/pittsburghtrib/s_61798.html

Appendix A

Downey, C., & Steffy, B. (Eds.). (2009). *Generally accepted audit principles for curriculum management (and Addendum)*. Johnston, IA: Curriculum Management Systems, Inc. (CMSi).

Additional Suggested Reading

American Association of School Administrators, National Association of Elementary School Principals, and National Association of Secondary School Principals. (1988). *School-based management: A strategy for better learning*. Washington, DC: AASA Publications.

Cuban, L. (1988). *The managerial imperative and the practice of leadership in schools*. Albany, NY: SUNY Press.

Goodlad, J. I. (1984). *A place called school: Prospects for the future*. New York: McGraw-Hill.

National Commission on Excellence in Education (1983). *A nation at risk: The imperative for educational reform*. Washington, DC: U.S. Department of Education.

Poston, W. K. (1990). Curriculum-driven budgeting: Case study of a recent approach to quality control. *National Forum of Educational Administration and Supervision Journal, 7*(2), 59–69.

Poston, W. K. (1991, January). *Curriculum-driven budgeting: Using educational priorities in school budgets*. Paper presented at a seminar of the National Academy for School Executives, San Diego, CA.

Poston, W. K. (2005). Finance, planning, and budgeting. In F. English (Ed.), *The Sage handbook of educational leadership: Advances in theory, research, and practice*, (Part V, pp. 550–570). Thousand Oaks, CA: Sage.

Swanson, A. D., & King, R. A. (1991). *School finance: Its economics and politics*. New York: Longman.

Wood, R. C. (Ed.). (1986). *Principles of school business management*. Reston, VA: Association for School Business Officials.

Index

CORWIN

A SAGE Company

The Corwin logo—a raven striding across an open book—represents the union of courage and learning. Corwin is committed to improving education for all learners by publishing books and other professional development resources for those serving the field of PreK–12 education. By providing practical, hands-on materials, Corwin continues to carry out the promise of its motto: **"Helping Educators Do Their Work Better."**